HOW TO
MAXIMISE
YOUR LIFE

BRIAN HOUSTON

HOW TO MAXIMISE YOUR LIFE

A compiled and revised edition of the five books
How to Live a Blessed Life,
How to Build Great Relationships,
How to Flourish in Life,
How to Make Wise Choices
and
How to Live in Health & Wholeness

Published by Hillsong Music Australia

Published by Hillsong Music Australia
www.hillsongmusic.com | www.brianandbobbie.com
A: PO Box 1195 Castle Hill NSW 1765 Australia
T: +61 2 8853 5300
F: +61 2 8846 4625
E: resources@hillsong.com

Edited by Ruth Athanasio.
Cover photo by Glen Allsop.
Design by Daniel Lai.
Printed in Singapore by the OPUS Group.

CONTENTS

BOOK I. HOW TO LIVE A BLESSED LIFE
--- PRINCIPLES FROM THE LIFE OF THE RIGHTEOUS MAN IN PSALM 112

BOOK II. How to Build Great Relationships

--- PRINCIPLES FOR FRIENDSHIP AND PARTNERSHIP, MARRIAGE AND PARENTING

BOOK III. How to Flourish in Life
--- Principles for building a thriving, productive life

BOOK IV. How to Make Wise Choices
--- Principles for building a life of wisdom

BOOK V. How to Live in Health & Wholeness
--- Principles for health and wholeness in body, soul and spirit

CONTENTS

BOOK ONE

HOW TO LIVE A BLESSED LIFE

PRINCIPLES FROM THE LIFE OF THE RIGHTEOUS MAN IN PSALM 112

HOW TO MAXIMISE YOUR LIFE

Introduction

How to live a blessed life – I believe that is what every human being needs to know. Yet the reality is that there is already a book in existence that gives all the instruction you need. It is the most widely read, most often translated and best-selling book of all time. If you haven't guessed it, that book is the Bible.

There are some who think that the Bible is dull and irrelevant, full of rules and regulations. Sadly, that presumption causes them to miss out on the wealth of truth, information and understanding about God and life that the Bible contains.

As God's Word to us, it has all the wisdom we need for living life successfully. It covers everything – from health, finance, business and work, to relationships, marriage and parenting – anything and everything you could ever want to know. No matter how many times you read it, there is always something new and relevant for whatever circumstance you are facing.

The Bible is my manual for living. It embraces every aspect of life and I've given my life to teaching its principles to others.

Among the diverse range of colourful characters in the Old Testament, there is one I particularly admire and aspire to most of all. I love his thinking and approach to life. His name isn't mentioned, but he lives by Bible principles and in ten verses of scripture, you read how God's blessing crosses the spectrum of his life.

This Bible hero of mine is the righteous man described in Psalm 112, and by applying some of the key principles with which he conducts his life, we can live a blessed life too.

PSALM 112

¹ Praise the LORD!

Blessed *is* the man *who* fears the LORD,
Who delights greatly in His commandments.

² His descendants will be mighty on earth;
The generation of the upright will be blessed.
³ Wealth and riches *will* be in his house,
And his righteousness endures forever.
⁴ Unto the upright there arises light in the darkness;
He is gracious, and full of compassion, and
righteous.
⁵ A good man deals graciously and lends;
He will guide his affairs with discretion.
⁶ Surely he will never be shaken;
The righteous will be in everlasting remembrance.
⁷ He will not be afraid of evil tidings;
His heart is steadfast, trusting in the LORD.
⁸ His heart *is* established;
He will not be afraid,
Until he sees *his desire* upon his enemies.

⁹ He has dispersed abroad,
He has given to the poor;
His righteousness endures forever;
His horn will be exalted with honor.
¹⁰ The wicked will see *it* and be grieved;
He will gnash his teeth and melt away;
The desire of the wicked shall perish.

Praise the Lord!
'Praise the LORD!' (Psalm 112:1)

Praise the Lord! Within those three words is the powerful beginning and foundation of a blessed life. It starts with knowing who God is and praising Him.

Praise is always a starting point. It means thankfulness – that is why we give thanks before a meal and start church with songs of praise. Jesus began to thank God before Lazarus was raised from the dead, and Moses praised God before He parted the Red Sea. Human nature likes to wait until after an answer is received, but blessing begins with praise.

The Word of God tells us to, 'Enter into His gates with thanksgiving, *And* into His courts with praise' (Psalm 100:4). Yet praising the Lord is not limited to singing a few songs once a week in a church service. Worship is a lifestyle that embraces the entire spectrum of life. You can praise God at any hour of the day, seven days a week – in the car, in the shower or in the middle of night. It isn't about singing a particular hymn or reciting a prayer – it's about a relationship with your Heavenly Father who loves and cares for you.

People have different ideas of what God is like and they communicate with Him according to their perception. Those who think He is rigid and austere keep their distance. Others who see Him as formal and stiff, usually approach Him in the same way. Yet those who know Him as Father and Friend enjoy the blessing of a close, intimate relationship with Him – where you can call on Him any time.

No matter what situation you may be in, you are not alone. Circumstances begin to turn around when you start praising God. Not only does it put Him in focus, but it causes you to see things from a whole new perspective. When He becomes the focus of your life, things begin to change for the better.

Blessing

'...Blessed *is* the man *who* fears the LORD...' (Psalm 112:1)

'Blessed (happy, fortunate, to be envied) is the man who fears (reveres and worships) the Lord' is the way the Amplified Bible translates the first verse of Psalm 112. Throughout the Bible, God consistently promises to bless His people, but His blessing also depends on our choices. He puts two clear choices before people: 'I have set before you life and death, blessing and cursing; therefore choose life, that both you and your descendants may live;' (Deuteronomy 30:19)

The book of Deuteronomy in the Old Testament contains a list of blessings and a list of curses which were directly linked to whether one chose to obey or disobey the commandments of the Lord. You can read these in Deuteronomy 28:1-14. To choose life with God is to choose a blessed life.

God's will is always to bless you, but if you think His blessing is entirely for you, you are missing the point. The blessing of God in your life should go well beyond your own existence. God told Abraham that He would bless him, but the purpose of blessing him went far beyond his own life. This is what God said:

'I will make you a great nation;
I will bless you
And make your name great;
And you shall be a blessing.'
(Genesis 12:2)

The purpose of God's blessing is to enable you to be a great channel of blessing to others. If you have nothing, there is nothing you can do for anyone else; if you have a little, you can only help a little; but if you have plenty, there is a whole lot you can do. When you are blessed, you have a mighty foundation from which to impact others. You are blessed to be a blessing.

The Word

'...Who delights greatly in His commandments.' (Psalm 112:1)

You will only enjoy the Bible's promises if you choose to live by Bible principles. Everyone wants to be blessed, but not everyone is prepared to live by the conditions or principles that bring about God's blessing. Simply put, if you want Bible results, you have to live by Bible principles.

Psalm 112 tells us that the righteous man 'delights greatly' in God's commandments. He loves the Word of God and has made it the foundation on which he builds his life. The result is a life which is a candidate for blessing in every area – relationships, finance, career, social life, family and spiritual life.

Living according to God's Word is not a selective process that allows you to choose to live by some commandments but not others. The Bible says:

> 'This Book of the Law shall not depart from your mouth, but you shall meditate in it day and night, that you may observe to do according to all that is written in it. For then you will make your way prosperous, and then you will have good success.' (Joshua 1:8)

If you want to live a blessed life, understand that the key is to observe to do according to all that is written in the Bible. One might be impressed with someone who knows what the Bible says, but it is much more impressive to see its promises actively blessing someone's life.

The blessed man in Psalm 112 took delight in God's Word because he saw it working in his life. In the New Testament, James encourages us to 'be doers of the word, and not hearers only' (James 1:22). You can faithfully 'attend' church or listen to sermons but unless you apply the principles, you will not experience the kind of blessing God intends for your life.

Impact and Influence

'His descendants will be mighty on earth...' (Psalm 112:2)

Your life is a lot bigger than you might think it is. Not only are you blessed to be a blessing to others, but you are also setting the pattern or example which others will follow. The Apostle Paul wrote to Timothy saying: 'Hold fast the pattern of sound words which you have heard from me, in faith and love which are in Christ Jesus.' (2 Timothy 1:13)

By building his life according to God's principles, the righteous man in Psalm 112 established the course for his 'descendants to be mighty on the earth.' This speaks of a people who are strong, influential and making a difference in the world. Have you ever stopped to consider the pattern your life is setting for the generations following you? The Bible says:

'A good *man* leaves an inheritance for his children's children...'
(Proverbs 13:22)

A great legacy to leave your children or grandchildren goes way beyond a house or a lump sum of money. A great legacy is the successful example of your life, which enables them to build on the foundation you have laid. Our capacity to live powerful and effective lives can transcend our own and impact future generations.

'I have been young, and *now* am old;
Yet I have not seen the righteous forsaken,
Nor his descendants begging bread.
He is ever merciful, and lends;
And his descendants *are* blessed.'
(Psalm 37:25-26)

The promise of God for a righteous life is that the blessing on your life will be passed on to your descendants.

Generations

'The generation of the upright will be blessed.' (Psalm 112:2)

God always works through generations. From generation to generation, blessing and curses are being passed on. Look back at your own family tree, and you may discover what blessings (or problems and negative characteristics, for that matter) you have inherited.

The good news is that no matter what your background or heritage, not only can you change the course of your life, but you can set a new course for the generations ahead. The moment you give your life to Jesus Christ is the moment a new spiritual heritage begins. The Bible says:

'Train up a child in the way he should go,
And when he is old he will not depart from it.'
(Proverbs 22:6)

A child will grow up in the way they were trained or raised. This works both positively and negatively. You can see the fruit of Biblical principles when they become the foundation of a young person's life. They have purpose, confidence, great attitudes and are becoming successful. On the other hand, you can see the deterioration of generations when Christ and His principles are rejected or compromised.

The choices you make today have the power to change the future. The righteous man in Psalm 112 imparted something powerful to his children – the wisdom and principles of God that enabled them to live blessed lives.

When you live according to God's principles, you are passing on God's blessing to future generations.

Abundance
'Wealth and riches *will* be in his house...' (Psalm 112:3)

Another promise of God is that wealth and riches will be in your house. I know there are those who would be more comfortable if the verse said wealth and riches will be in his heart rather than in his house. They are the ones who wrestle with the fact that abundance is the promise of God for their lives.

It is amazing that so many Christians struggle with the idea of having plenty. Sadly, this kind of thinking has held the Church back because it presumes that wealth and greed are the same thing, and this limits resourcefulness. 'Prosperity' is a word frequently found in the Bible; so are the words 'blessing', 'wealth', 'riches' and 'abundance.' I cannot find any scripture that states it is God's will for us to be poor and destitute. For instance, the Word of God says:

> "'Let the LORD be magnified,
> Who has pleasure in the prosperity of His servant.'" (Psalm 35:27)

Think about that – God rejoices when we we are doing well. The impact of our success is enlarged and finds its purpose when we get the revelation that His blessing in our lives has others as its focus.

Our Heavenly Father, like any loving parent, does not mind if His children are financially blessed. But bear in mind that wealth and riches are just one aspect of an abundant life – it goes further than material goods. John wrote: 'Beloved, I pray that you may prosper in all things and be in health, just as your soul prospers.' (3 John 1:2)

Money cannot buy family, great relationships, a good reputation or your physical well-being. Don't under-estimate or exclude these blessings from your definition of abundance. A truly prosperous person desires the fullness of God in every area of their life.

Righteousness

'...And his righteousness endures forever.' (Psalm 112:3)

Never lose sight of the fact that God desires to bless you. It is interesting to note how often 'righteousness' and the principles of blessing are mentioned together in the Bible. Simply put, righteousness means to be in right standing with God.

I don't believe money is a problem with God because it is a tremendous resource for good – but the Bible consistently confronts a person's attitude towards money. It says that 'the love of money is the root of all *kinds* of evil' (1 Timothy 6:10). The purposes of your heart will distinguish whether what you do with your money has the potential for righteousness or unrighteousness. The Word of God says:

> 'For no sooner has the sun risen with a burning heat than it withers the grass; its flower falls, and its beautiful appearance perishes. So the rich man also will fade away in his pursuits.' (James 1:11)

The problem isn't in the rich man's wealth, but in what his heart is pursuing. If your pursuits are focusing only on your needs and your desires, then they are temporal and will fade away. But Jesus instructed us quite clearly about what we should pursue: 'But seek first the kingdom of God and His righteousness, and all these things shall be added to you.' (Matthew 6:33)

The key here is what you put FIRST and what are your priorities in life. When you put God's Kingdom first in your life and pursue His righteousness, His promise is that 'these things' – your material needs such as food or clothing – will be met. Making His Kingdom your priority means you sow into something that has eternal value and will not fade away. As the Bible declares, '...and His righteousness endures forever.'

Help in Trouble

'Unto the upright there arises light in the darkness...' (Psalm 112:4)

We will all face challenges in our lives – be it financial pressures, work and health issues, or relationship challenges. One of the great blessings in life is that no matter what we are going through, we are never alone. The Bible says:

'God *is* our refuge and strength,
A very present help in trouble.' (Psalm 46:1)

King David, the writer of 'The Lord is my shepherd,' knew the 'present help' of God. In Psalm 23, he wrote, 'though I walk through the valley of the shadow of death, I will fear no evil; For You *are* with me.' He also wrote, 'My heart also instructs me in the night seasons' (Psalm 16:7).

There are many things that thrive in the darkness of night, such as confusion, anxiety and fear. Many have lost their way in dark times, but the promise to the righteous man in Psalm 112 is that in the midst of darkness, there arises a light. Throughout the Bible, the analogy of light is always representative of God. Jesus is called the Light of the world, and light always dispels the darkness.

Our challenge is to stand strong and remain consistent when we face the 'dark times.' If, as David said, it is our heart that instructs us in these times, then we need to set our heart on the promises of God. If all your heart knows is panic, then that is the instruction it will give you, and you will feel helpless and powerless in a time of trouble.

In the midst of a crisis, remain faithful and diligent. Stand firmly on the Word of God, ask Him to guide you, and you will eventually see the darkness disperse. Remember, God is 'a very present help in trouble.'

Grace and Compassion

'...*He is* gracious, and full of compassion, and righteous.' (Psalm 112:4)

The righteous man in Psalm 112 is described as someone who is gracious and full of compassion. These two powerful qualities are also attributes of Jesus Christ. You may have heard the words of the well-known song *Amazing Grace* and wondered what was so amazing about grace? God's grace is His favour, cannot be earned and is bountiful in supply. It is a free gift. Some people can't accept that grace is enough – they want to do something more to earn it themselves.

'...where sin abounded, grace abounded much more...'
(Romans 5:20)

You may have made some big mistakes in your life, but these do not have to dominate your future if you understand that God's grace prevails even more. There is nothing more you need to do, other than make the decision to turn your life around and accept His unmerited favour and undeserved blessing. When you have an understanding of God's grace, you can accept His blessing in your life.

Compassion is another powerful characteristic. Every time Jesus was moved with compassion, something powerful happened. 'And when Jesus went out He saw a great multitude; and He was moved with compassion for them...' (Matthew 14:14)

When facing a tough situation, human nature is easily drawn to sympathy, but the reality is that sympathy is not always what is needed. Sympathy identifies with the problem or hurt, and may make you feel better for a time, but it is not focussed on helping you move forward.

People tend to surround themselves with those who 'understand them' or 'accept them just the way they are,' rather than positioning themselves in a challenging environment that will direct them towards answers. Sympathy doesn't have any answers, but compassion is a powerful force that activates God's answers for your life.

Dealing Graciously

'A good man deals graciously and lends...' (Psalm 112:5)

God's promise is that we should be the lender and not the borrower (see Deuteronomy 28:12). If you are always in need, you are poorly positioned to help others. It is far better to be well positioned to lend or give to others, than to constantly be on the receiving end. The Bible describes it in this way:

> 'The rich rules over the poor,
> And the borrower *is* servant to the lender.' (Proverbs 22:7)

Commit yourself to a journey in which you progress from being the borrower or the receiver, to being the lender or supplier. Ownership puts you in a position to bless other people's lives – it gives you this opportunity because you cannot give what you do not own. It isn't about you controlling others but protecting you from being the subject of manipulation or control. If you are always taking or borrowing, it imprisons or binds you, but when you are in the position to give, it releases you.

While the world is often on the take with ruthless wheelings and dealings, a Godly person should act fairly and be gracious in their dealings. This includes the way they do business, and the way they deal with people and relationships. It also affects the way they respond to hurt and offences.

If you want to know how to deal graciously, just think about how God deals with those who choose to follow Him – with an immeasurable supply of grace. When it comes to relationships or business, make a commitment to be open and honest. The blessing of God doesn't include shady dealings or dishonesty. Have integrity when it comes to finances, and treat others with grace and generosity. Working within the right principles and parameters will not only bless you, but those you deal with will experience the blessing too.

Guided by Discretion

'...He will guide his affairs with discretion.' (Psalm 112:5)

The Word says that the Psalm 112 man guides his affairs with discretion. To be guided means to be directed, led or steered towards a specific course. Some people aren't guided by anything – they are tossed around by circumstances, but Jesus said: '...when He, the Spirit of truth, has come, He will guide you into all truth...' (John 16:13)

There will always be many options available to you in life, but God's way will always steer you in the direction of His purposes. Why should you be guided by discretion? The Word of God says:

'Discretion will preserve you;
Understanding will keep you.' (Proverbs 2:11)

Discretion will keep you on course. Conducting your affairs with discretion will protect you from the consequences of hasty or bad decisions. It includes dealing graciously, having integrity and using Godly wisdom.

To have discretion also means to be blessed with good taste and good sense. There are some who have great taste but no sense, and others who have good sense but no taste. For example, if you were to buy a beautiful luxury car which you couldn't afford – you have great taste but no sense. (Some choose a car which shows good sense but no taste!) A young man's choice of a beautiful bride may show impeccable taste, but if he ignores or mistreats her, he lacks good sense. He'll never have the marriage he dreams about.

I believe you can have both by guiding your affairs according to the Word of God and listening to your conscience. Approach your life wisely, with good judgement, and live a life of blessing.

Unshakeable
'Surely he will never be shaken...' (Psalm 112:6)

One of the certainties in the life of the Psalm 112 man is that he will 'never be shaken.' It doesn't say that he won't experience times of 'shaking' but the promise of God is that he won't be shaken loose. Why? Because he is firmly fixed in position, or as these verses say, his heart is steadfast and established.

How easily can you be shaken? The truth is you will never know until you feel the shaking. In December 1989, a destructive earthquake hit the New South Wales city of Newcastle. I had stayed there on occasion in a particular modern hotel, but after the earthquake, that building ceased to exist. On the outside, it appeared to be the building least likely to fall in an earthquake, but it was completely ruined.

Why is it that some people are destroyed by shaky times and others emerge strong and victorious? It all depends on where their heart is set and established. The psalmist wrote:

> 'I have set the LORD always before me;
> Because *He is* at my right hand I shall not be moved.' (Psalm 16:8)

In the same way a plane flies according to a set computerised flight plan, your life operates according to the way your heart is set. When you are feeling disappointment or your faith is being tested, what is inside your heart will come out. If your heart is not set or established on the right foundation, your life will veer off course.

What you really believe will come out in the midst of adversity. Jesus said that from the abundance of the heart the mouth speaks. It is easy to sing praises to God and speak positively when everything is going well, but what comes out when you are facing a crisis? When your heart is established and set according to God's Word, you may feel tremors along the way, but you won't be shaken loose or go off course.

Lasting Legacy

'...The righteous will be in everlasting remembrance.' (Psalm 112:6)

Have you ever wondered what kind of name you will leave behind when you have departed from this earth? A good name, a bad name, or no name?

Leaving behind a good name for your children is a great inheritance, instead of the liability of a bad name with a bad reputation. Your name is something your descendants should be proud to bear and wear like a badge of honour. The Word says:

> 'The memory of the righteous *is* blessed,
> But the name of the wicked will rot.' (Proverbs 10:7)

Earlier, we looked at the power of impacting the future generations, but in serving the future, we cannot neglect to serve the present.

A blessed life is one that understands that when God saves you, He has others in mind. I believe every Christian needs to know that they are not only saved, but are also called to live a life of purpose.

> '[God] who has saved us and called us with a holy calling...'
> (2 Timothy 1:9)

One of the greatest things we can contribute to in our lives is in building what Jesus said He would build – His Church. He said the gates of hell will not prevail against His Church, so our commitment to the establishment and success of His Church brings our life into line with His will.

One of the greatest decisions you can make is to choose to live a life that is dedicated to accomplishing and building something that will stand as a testimony or legacy for the generations ahead.

No Worries
'He will not be afraid of evil tidings...' (Psalm 112:7)

I once taught a series of messages entitled 'What a worry worry is.' It is amazing how much time people spend worrying – about their work, relationships, money or health.

Do you know that the very sound of a telephone ringing can strike fear into the heart of a person who is fearful of bad news, and cause their heart to sink? Inevitably, that anxiety will begin to rule their life and affect them physically, emotionally and spiritually. The truth is that worry will always hold you back and limit your potential. It never produces anything positive, because it always focuses on the problem instead of the answers. This is what the Bible says:

'Anxiety in the heart of man causes depression,
But a good word makes it glad.' (Proverbs 12:25)

In the face of life's challenges, surround yourself with positive, faith-filled words that challenge the problem and focus on answers. Your environment is critical at such times. Carefully choose your friends, your counsel, and your place of worship. Avoid those whose belief system is devoid of answers for life's everyday problems. Never accept the mindset that persecution and suffering are the will of God; they are the weapons of the devil who is hell-bent on distracting you from God's amazing plan for your life. While he would prefer you to become consumed with negativity, it is the will of God for you to fill your life with a good report.

Anxiety, worry and fear will rob you of faith and hope, and ultimately prevent you from moving forward with God. The words 'Do not fear' are a frequent instruction in scripture, and it says 'be anxious for nothing' (Philippians 4:6). If you are living according to God's principles of peace and blessing, you need never be afraid of bad news. Even when a bad report comes, it will not rule your life.

Steadfastness and Trust

'...His heart is steadfast, trusting in the LORD.' (Psalm 112:7)

One of the advantages of having a vibrant faith is steadfastness. To be steadfast involves a refusal to be swayed or moved from your course. It is sheer determination and the ability to stand firm against all odds. You don't have to live on an emotional roller coaster if your life is founded on a genuine faith in God.

The first pastor of the Corinthian Church was the Apostle Paul who challenged the early Christians to be steadfast: '...be steadfast, immovable, always abounding in the work of the Lord, knowing that your labor is not in vain...' (1 Corinthians 15:58)

The first century Christians stood firm in the midst of persecution, and as a result, they experienced tremendous increase and progress. Psalm 112 links steadfastness to trusting God. The righteous man in Psalm 112 has great wealth and riches, but his heart isn't trusting in them – his trust is in the Lord. Faith and trust such as this will produce steadfastness and stability in your life.

To put your trust in someone or something means you will have a firm belief in their reliability, and a confident expectation that they will not let you down. Such dependability is the outcome of a vibrant relationship with the Almighty God. He is called El Shaddai, which means 'All sufficient one' – ever dependable, always steadfast. He is the foundation of a steadfast spirit that will cause you to be forward-focused and immovably persistent. This is what the Bible says:

> 'Trust in the LORD with all your heart,
> And lean not on your own understanding;
> In all your ways acknowledge Him,
> And He shall direct your paths.' (Proverbs 3:5-6)

When you trust God with your whole life, you need never be anxious or afraid. He will never let you down.

Convictions

'His heart *is* established;' (Psalm 112:8)

You may wonder why there are those whose lives follow a pattern of crisis and inconsistency, while others live according to a pattern of blessing and good fortune. It's simple – those with strong convictions build strength into their life, but those who have weak convictions, weaken their lives. It all depends where one's heart is set.

The truth is, if you stand for nothing, you will fall for anything! You cannot be neutral – you have to make a stand. The Apostle Paul knew what he stood for, and nothing could sway him from his convictions. From his prison cell, he wrote of what he knew and believed, of his persuasion and commitment to Jesus Christ.

> '...nevertheless I am not ashamed, for I know whom I have believed and am persuaded that He is able to keep what I have committed to Him until that Day.' (2 Timothy 1:12)

There are many who don't know what their convictions are – they are unsure about what they believe. Instead of being influential or persuasive, they are easily influenced by whatever comes their way. Your persuasion or convictions determine your course in life. The result is that you will either be someone who lives with conviction, or someone who lives by consequence.

> 'There is a way *that seems* right to a man,
> But its end *is* the way of death.' (Proverbs 16:25)

A lack of conviction will not kill you physically, but it may lead to the death of your dreams, your marriage or your well-being. Living by consequence means putting your trust in what seems right, but living with conviction is living according to what is right – living God's way! You need to know what your convictions are because they are the beliefs and principles that will establish a pattern for your life.

Success

'He will not be afraid, Until he sees his desire
upon his enemies.' (Psalm 112:8)

A blessed life is one that will know success, not failure. Success, like prosperity, is a Bible word. In Joshua 1:8, the promise of God is that living by the principles of the Bible will 'make your way prosperous, and then you will have good success.' As discussed earlier, to achieve that success means meditating on the Word of God and living according to His principles.

Some people think it is a formula – that God will wave a magic wand and they will begin to prosper. However, you cannot approach the blessing of God with some sort of penny-in-the-slot mentality, thinking, 'If I do this, God has to do that.'

Some people become discouraged when they don't see breakthrough immediately, but the faithfulness of God isn't proven in a week or a month. You need to have a life-long approach to His principles.

You may look at some well-known, successful people and want what they have. But instead of only looking at their position now, you need to consider what it took to get them there. Many people want the blessing and promise, but they don't want to work for it or wait for it. The Word of God says: '...imitate those who through faith and patience inherit the promises.' (Hebrews 6:12)

Many people with great potential have sabotaged their opportunity because they lacked the patience to endure in the tough times. You will need staying-power if you want to live a blessed life. If you don't experience success straight away, don't give up. Keep on doing the will of God with a spirit of patience and endurance. He has given you all you need to fulfill His plan and purpose for your life, and if you constantly put God first, you can trust Him to fulfill His promise to bless you.

Vision

'He has dispersed abroad...' (Psalm 112:9)

One of the things I love about this righteous man in Psalm 112 is that he clearly lives a life that goes well beyond himself. When it says, 'he has dispersed abroad,' it speaks of one whose life has a far-reaching and wide-ranging impact on others.

There are those who never seem to move forward in life because their vision is small. Instead of continuing to grow and expand their life, they prefer to be a big fish in a small pond. In doing so, they limit their own potential. The Bible says:

'Where there is no vision, the people perish...'
(Proverbs 29:18 KJV)

Having a dream or specific goal will add direction and purpose to your life. There are so many people who are frustrated because they aren't going anywhere or achieving anything. Their time, their energy and their finance is wasted because their life lacks purpose.

In my book *For This I Was Born*, I wrote about the words of Jesus – He knew that He was born for the Cause of God's Kingdom, and understood that His connection to the world revolved around that Cause. You and I are also born for the Cause, which involves living a life with influence that goes well beyond ourselves.

It is easy to get caught up in the stress and pressure of your job, working to pay the bills and to put food on your table. But with a big-hearted spirit, you begin to think about dispersing abroad in terms of what you can do for others, and putting food on many other tables. It is impossible to have a vision that is bigger than God's plans for your life. His plans are HUGE. As God begins to bless your life, keep expanding and looking beyond yourself to build His Kingdom. The world is your oyster!

Generosity

'He has given to the poor...' (Psalm 112:9)

God's nature is to give, and everything He does comes from a generous spirit. In the same way, we should desire to be truly generous and allow our lives to be a flow of blessing to others. Generosity isn't about how much you have, nor is it proven in a single act – the true spirit of generosity is a lifestyle.

• A way of seeing

'He who has a generous eye will be blessed,
For he gives of his bread to the poor.' (Proverbs 22:9)

A generous eye will see beyond itself and quickly spot opportunities to bless others. Instead of being someone who sits back and makes harsh judgements about others, a generous spirit will be open to believe the best.

• A way of thinking

'But a generous man devises generous things...' (Isaiah 32:8)

When generosity is a way of thinking, one will always be devising plans to bless others. God saw the need of the world and He devised a generous strategy. It is called the Gospel, which means 'good news.'

• A way of living

'And by generosity he shall stand.' (Isaiah 32:8)

When generosity is a way of living, it becomes our stance. It is not a labour, a single action or a grudging obligation – it is a way of life. The promise of God is that one who has a 'generous eye' is someone who will be blessed themselves.

God's Kingdom refers to everything within His realm, both in Heaven and on earth. To have a Kingdom spirit means you have a vision that is bigger than you – you will always be devising generous strategies or plans to bless others. Generosity will be a way of seeing, a way of thinking, and a way of living.

Endurance

'His righteousness endures forever...' (Psalm 112:9)

The promises of God are readily available to you, but you will need a commitment to endurance, persistence and patience to see them established. The Bible tells us: 'For you have need of endurance, so that after you have done the will of God, you may receive the promise...' (Hebrews 10:36)

Endurance is about the refusal to surrender, and the determination to keep on going until you receive the promise. Once you decide you want to live a life built on the principles of God, you may face opposition and persecution, as well as the temptation to quit. James wrote: 'Blessed *is* the man who endures temptation; for when he has been approved, he will receive the crown of life...' (James 1:12)

The Bible is full of encouragement to stand strong in the face of adversity. James continued in his letter, pointing out that 'when' we are tempted (not if), it does not come from God. He went on to describe how temptation starts when people are enticed by their own desires, or quite literally, deceitful representations, which paint an unrealistic picture that does not exist. My wife Bobbie and I once visited Florence in Italy, and when we checked into our hotel, the room looked nothing like the one in the brochure. When querying this, the hotel front desk told us, 'That's just a picture' – the room did not exist!

In the face of discouragement, be wary of illusions that form in your mind which make quitting or compromising look attractive. Such a picture does not tell the whole story and is part of Satan's strategy to rob you of God's blessing. A spirit of endurance is about commitment to the long haul – and you will need it when it comes to your marriage, your finances and even your spiritual walk with God. When the going gets tough, don't look for short-cuts or the easy way out.

Respect

'His horn will be exalted with honor.' (Psalm 112:9)

Psalm 112 describes how the righteous man's 'horn will be exalted with honour.' In Bible terms, his 'horn' refers to his strength and influence, and to be 'honoured' is all about others recognising his value. It literally means that his influence is elevated through credibility and respect, causing him to rise to great influence and a place of honour.

It is clear that respect is part of God's blessing, and is a tremendous advantage in living a life of influence. The Word says that Godly wisdom will lead to '...favor and high esteem in the sight of God and man.' (Proverbs 3:4)

Think about what it means to have favour and to be held in high esteem by both God and others. Such a person would be one who had good character and great influence.

So why would respect be a blessing in your life? You can be successful in what you do, but without respect, you can never reach any significant level of influence. Here are five things respect will add to your life:

- Your words will have authority.
- Success will follow you.
- Promotion will be a way of life.
- Respect will protect you from rumours and attack.
- People will rally to your cause.

Respect is not a luxury that can be bought. It is not something you can demand, but rather something you earn over time. The truth is that if you want to gain respect, you need to give respect. No matter what God has called you to do, giving honour and gaining respect will help you achieve it.

Protection
'The wicked will see *it* and be grieved...' (Psalm 112:10)

Respect will protect you against unexpected attacks from your adversaries. For centuries, one of Satan's strategies has been to destroy the credibility of Christians and undermine the reputation of the Church.

Losing your credibility can render you ineffective because you can also lose the authority, blessing and position of influence you may have gained. Having integrity, righteousness and respect are a great protection against the weapons of your enemy, the devil. The promise in the Word of God is:

'No weapon formed against you shall prosper,
And every tongue *which* rises against you in judgement
You shall condemn.
This *is* the heritage of the servants of the LORD.' (Isaiah 54:17)

Weapons may be formed against you, but they certainly won't be successful, unless you make yourself an easy target. The Bible clearly instructs us: 'nor give place to the devil.' (Ephesians 4:27)

Giving him no opportunity, no advantage and no permission to move in your life is how you thwart his attempts to rob you of the blessing of God.

To be a skillful tennis player, you have to cut off the angles, making it difficult for your opponent to get a shot past you. This is how you can counter the strategies of the devil – cut off the angles and don't be ignorant of his devices. Satan will never play fair. If there are issues in your life that give him room to move, deal with them. If you don't, you are giving him opportunity to use them against you. You can close the door on him and bullet-proof your marriage, your emotions, your health and your finances by living according to God's principles.

Persecution

'He will gnash his teeth and melt away...' (Psalm 112:10)

I mentioned earlier how the Amplified Bible describes 'blessed' as 'happy, fortunate and to be envied.' The reality is that when God begins to bless your life, not everyone will be happy about it.

The blessing of God is enviable and can cause some to 'gnash their teeth.' Along with the blessing of abundance and success, you can expect to face opposition. When you put God first, this is what Jesus said you can expect:

> 'Assuredly, I say to you, there is no one who has left house or brothers or sisters or father or mother or wife or children or lands, for My sake and the gospel's, who shall not receive a hundredfold now in this time – houses and brothers and sisters and mothers and children and lands, with persecutions – and in the age to come, eternal life.' (Mark 10:29-30)

When we make a stand for God, we should never be surprised if we attract opposition or persecution. The devil is always seeking to steal, kill and destroy, but persecution will also come from a minority who feel threatened by God's blessing. For instance, Jesus faced persecution from kings who thought their kingdom was under threat, from crowds who realised their mediocrity was threatened, and religious leaders who sensed their legalistic beliefs were under threat. A blessed life will attract attention from those who will attempt to pull you down to size – their size!

When your life is impacted by God, you clearly have what others want. In the midst of persecution, refuse to draw back or allow others to rule your spirit. 'Having done all, stand' and keep your course.

Victory

'The desire of the wicked shall perish.' (Psalm 112:10)

The final sentence that describes the life of the righteous man in Psalm 112 states that 'the desire of the wicked shall perish' or come to nothing. In other words, the desire (or plans and purposes) of God will stand. What a triumphant conclusion to a blessed life! The promise in God's Word is: '...He who has begun a good work in you will complete *it* unto the day of Jesus Christ;' (Philippians 1:6)

God is committed to seeing you succeed and He desires to complete what He has started in your life. Your faith will be tested and there will be times when you will face the temptation to abandon the principles of God, but the key is to take on the spirit of an overcomer. This is how an overcomer will approach life: 'And let us not grow weary while doing good, for in due season we shall reap if we do not lose heart.' (Galatians 6:9)

This verse reveals five characteristics of an overcomer:

• **They refuse to grow weary.** At times they may be physically tired yet they are still energised by vision, focus and opportunity in life.

• **They continue to do good.** Whether or not they have a good start, an overcomer will be determined to finish well.

• **They recognise their season is due** (perhaps even overdue).

• **They are committed to reaping,** according to the good seed they have sown. Sow good seed and you can expect to reap accordingly.

• **An overcomer is determined not to lose heart.**

The adversary's plan is to hold you back from the blessing of God, and prevent you from reaching your goal and living a quality life. But John encourages us that 'He who is in you is greater than he who is in the world' (1 John 4:4).

42

Epilogue

I'm sure you will agree with me that the lifestyle of the righteous man in Psalm 112 is one we should all aspire to. The principles and commandments of God are evident right across the spectrum of his life. He has it all.

He puts God first in his life, he lives according to the Bible and as a result he is successful and blessed. He also has a far-sighted sense of purpose that extends well beyond himself. He gives generously to others; his family is blessed; he is making his mark and he is highly respected. Like anyone else, he faces his share of tests, trials, challenges and temptations, but he comes through victorious.

But there is more... not only is his life blessed, but his character is outstanding. He loves God, he is righteous, generous, just, gracious, compassionate, wise and full of integrity. He is someone we would all be drawn to and aspire to be like. Yet there is one final truth about this man.

When you turn over the page, you will read the psalm that precedes Psalm 112. Psalm 111 is a wonderful description of the awesome nature and character of God, but the amazing thing is that the psalmist has used exactly the same phrases to describe the character of the righteous man in Psalm 112. Not only does the righteous man experience blessing in every area of his life but his character is likened to God's – 'gracious', 'full of compassion' with a 'righteousness that endures forever.'

This righteous, blessed man may not be named, but I think there is a good reason for that. We all have the opportunity to be that person, and as we begin to live according to the principles of the Bible, we can put our own name to those ten verses.

May you live a blessed life.
Brian Houston

Psalm 111

¹ Praise the LORD!

I will praise the LORD with *my* whole heart,
In the assembly of the upright and *in* the congregation.

² The works of the LORD *are* great,
Studied by all who have pleasure in them.
³ His work *is* honorable and glorious,
And His righteousness endures forever.
⁴ He has made His wonderful works to be remembered;
The LORD *is* gracious and full of compassion.
⁵ He has given food to those who fear Him;
He will ever be mindful of His covenant.
⁶ He has declared to His people the power of His works,
In giving them the heritage of the nations.

⁷ The works of His hands *are* verity and justice;
All His precepts *are* sure.
⁸ They stand fast forever and ever,
And are done in truth and uprightness.
⁹ He has sent redemption to His people;
He has commanded His covenant forever:
Holy and awesome *is* His name.

¹⁰ The fear of the LORD *is* the beginning of wisdom;
A good understanding have all those who do *His commandments*.
His praise endures forever.

BOOK TWO

HOW TO BUILD GREAT RELATIONSHIPS

PRINCIPLES FOR FRIENDSHIP AND
PARTNERSHIP, MARRIAGE AND PARENTING

HOW TO MAXIMISE YOUR LIFE

Introduction

One of the greatest gifts God has given us is people. When you think of giving someone gifts, you may think of inanimate objects or things, but God thinks of people. When He saw Adam was alone, He gave him a wife and companion. When He saw the world in need, He gave us Jesus. When He wants to change an enterprise, community or nation, He raises up people who will fulfil His purposes.

Great relationships are a sign of a flourishing life but they don't come by chance. Sadly, we live in a world filled with broken relationships. I'm not only talking about broken marriages, but failed friendships, family fall-outs or bitter business partnerships. The reality is that you certainly don't fluke a good marriage, a great friendship or a successful business partnership. The principles that you sow into the relationship will determine what you reap.

Many take their relationships for granted and only when they experience problems, do they desperately seek answers or help. The truth is that if the pain and bitterness of one bad relationship is never dealt with, it has the potential to affect other relationships too. Yet the good news is that even those who have been hurt in intimate relationships can apply biblical principles, lay the right kind of foundations and go on to build great relationships.

So you want to know how to build great relationships? The Bible is the most comprehensive manual or handbook we have that contains all the principles we need for building successful relationships in every level of life. The Bible speaks about marriage, friendship, parenting, employer relations, leadership, how to treat others... and how to have a great relationship with God Himself.

THE POWER OF FRIENDSHIP

'Greater love has no one than this, than to lay down one's life for his friends. You are My friends if you do whatever I command you. No longer do I call you servants, for a servant does not know what his master is doing; but I have called you friends, for all things that I heard from My Father I have made known to you.' (John 15:13-15)

Loneliness
'It is not good that man should be alone...' (Genesis 2:18)

In the movie *Cast Away* actor Tom Hanks played a FedEx agent who was marooned on a remote Pacific island for four years. The need for friendship became so great that he kept himself sane by conversing with a volleyball he named 'Wilson'. Solitary confinement is one of the harshest measures of punishment for an individual. Good, intimate relationships will build up our lives, whereas isolation will break us down. In the beginning, God said: *'It is* not good that man should be alone...' (Genesis 2:18)

He created us to know the blessing of intimacy and within every one of us is the desire and need for companionship. Sadly, there are some who never seem to draw others into their lives. There is a proverb that says:

> 'A man who isolates himself seeks his own desire;
> He rages against all wise judgment.' (Proverbs 18:1)

This proverb describes a person who makes the choice to disconnect himself from others as 'seeking his own desire.' Instead of contributing to a relationship, such people are in it for their own gain, whether it be towards achieving a certain goal or needing constant approval and affirmation.

Why does such a person 'rage against all wise judgement'? People who are seeking their own desire inevitably make choices that support their particular pursuits. For example, someone who has an alcohol problem will gravitate towards drinking companions. Wise judgement would suggest that instead of relationships that support their weakness, they should seek to build friendships that strengthen and challenge them.

The starting point for building great relationships is making wise decisions about who we allow close to us. We need people who will build us up and take us forward, and good friends will do just that.

Building Great Friendships

'A man *who has* friends must himself be friendly...' (Proverbs 18:24)

Some of the most pleasurable moments in life are sitting around a table and sharing a meal with close friends. I'd consider friendship to be one of the key elements of a blessed life.

Thousands would crowd around Jesus to hear Him teach but it was His twelve companions who shared the most intimate moments of His life on earth. They were the ones who gathered together with Him in the upper room before His crucifixion, where He shared a table for twelve before the most challenging moment of His life. The Bible says:

'A man *who has* friends must himself be friendly...' (Proverbs 18:24)

There are those who never attract others into their lives. They miss the blessing of friendship because their attitude is more about what they can get instead of what they can give into the relationship. Just as we need to make deposits before we make withdrawals from our bank accounts, so we need to invest into our relationships. Another translation of Proverbs 18:24 illustrates a different aspect of friendship. It says:

'The man of many friends [a friend of all the world] will prove himself a bad friend...' (Proverbs 18:24 AMP)

There are many who want to be everyone's friend but they never become a true friend to anyone because they are not prepared to make a stand. Instead of giving a friend their whole-hearted support, they sit on the fence and try to be a friend to everyone.

A well-known personality in America who was sent to gaol for his fraudulent activities was once asked if he had lost any friends. His answer was profound. He stated that he didn't lose any friends but he found out who his friends really were. A true friend will stick with you during the good times and the bad times.

Loyalty and Love

'Greater love has no one than this, than to lay
down one's life for his friends.' (John 15:13)

How far would you go for a friend who is in trouble? Napoleon Bonaparte once made this observation: 'Alexander, Caesar, Charlemagne and myself founded great empires, but upon which did the creations of our genius depend? Upon force! Jesus alone founded His empire upon love, and to this very day, millions would die for Him!' Jesus said the following words: 'Greater love has no one than this, than to lay down one's life for his friends.' (John 15:13)

Jesus demonstrated His love by giving His life for us. He may have been betrayed by Judas, one of His twelve disciples, and Peter may have denied Him three times, but that didn't sway Him.

A friend is someone you love, and from whom you receive love. In ancient Greek and Latin, the word for friend ('philos' and 'amicus') is based on the word for love ('phile' and 'am'). The Bible describes a good friend in this way:

'A friend loves at all times' (Proverbs 17:17)

Loyalty and love are the attributes of true friends. Such friends will be there in season and out of season. They are the ones who rejoice when you are rejoicing, and will weep when you are weeping. Your close friends will know your weaknesses and strengths, and they will have watched you make mistakes, but they will be there to see you through the times of adversity.

The strength of a good friendship that goes the distance will be unconditional love. Such people won't stand by and be neutral when they hear criticism or gossip by busybodies behind the back of their friend. Their loyalty will cause them to make a stand and if called for, they will even put their own reputation on the line. They will believe in you no matter what happens, and will be committed to seeing you reach your potential in life.

A Friend to Your Destiny

'He who walks with wise *men* will be wise...' (Proverbs 13:20)

Are your friends the kind of people who take you forward and build you up? Wisdom in choosing your friends enables you to build relationships with those who will lift you up and support you. You cannot expect to achieve your best in life without other people, but a true friend will be a friend to your destiny. The Bible warns us of friendships that are potentially destructive in our lives: 'He who walks with wise *men* will be wise, But the companion of fools will be destroyed.' (Proverbs 13:20)

As the saying goes, birds of a feather flock together, and you will find that like-minded people tend to gravitate towards each other. For instance, negativity breeds negativity, and such people seem to gravitate towards others with a similar cynical attitude.

The reality is that the mentality or attitude of those you hang around with eventually rubs off on you. The psalmist wrote:

'I will set nothing wicked before my eyes;
I hate the work of those who fall away;
It shall not cling to me.' (Psalm 101:3)

The spirit of those around you will stick to you like glue. Be careful of wrong associations and what you allow to cling to you. Not everyone who appears friendly is a friend. The Bible describes how Satan approached Jesus in the wilderness with a seemingly friendly attitude, yet he was obviously not a friend to the purposes of God. His motive was to tempt Jesus to abandon God's plan. Yet good friends will have a positive influence in your life. There is a proverb that says:

'*As* iron sharpens iron,
So a man sharpens the countenance of his friend.' (Proverbs 27:17)

What rubs off on you will affect your future. Let the influence of your friends be one that sharpens and strengthens you the way iron sharpens iron.

Friendly Advice
'Faithful *are* the wounds of a friend...' (Proverbs 27:6)

Who do you turn to when you need good advice? In the same way that the spirit of your friends rubs off on you, so their counsel may cause you to make either good or bad decisions. A friend to your destiny is one who will sometimes tell you not what you want to hear but what you need to hear. The Bible says:

> 'Faithful *are* the wounds of a friend,
> But the kisses of an enemy *are* deceitful.' (Proverbs 27:6)

A friend will have the courage to be truthful with you, but always with your best interests at heart. When others may flatter you with compliments or cater to your sensitivities, a true friend will beautifully balance encouragement and honesty.

The suffering of the Old Testament character, Job, is well documented – he had lost his family, his fortune and his health. In the midst of it all, he was surrounded by counsel. There was his nagging wife and his three friends (or so-called comforters) who filled his ears with negativity and well-meaning advice. But Job refused to be swayed and firmly stood aloof from ungodly counsel. He spoke about: 'When the friendly counsel of God *was* over my tent;' (Job 29:4)

The counsel of God is available to us through the Bible and will always be a friend to our destiny. There may be times when His counsel may not seem to be that friendly or favourable towards your circumstances. The same way friends will always tell you when there is spinach between your teeth, God points out specific areas that we need to address in order to move forward.

Who we allow to speak into our lives is important. True friends will invest and inject something into your life that will build you up and take you forward.

The Test of Friendship

'...there is a friend *who* sticks closer than a brother.' (Proverbs 18:24)

When my two sons were growing up, they would fight each other (as brothers do) about petty things such as taking each other's socks. But they always stood up for each other if someone else was against them. There is a proverb that states:

> 'But there is a friend *who* sticks closer than a brother.'
> (Proverbs 18:24)

The kind of friendship that sticks closer than a brother is one that will endure anything. Not only will these friends be loyal and give you good counsel, but when the friendship is tested, they come through for you without fail. Friendships like these should be highly prized and guarded. Trust is a key element in such relationships, yet trust isn't gained overnight. It is always sad when two people who have been life-long friends fall out. The Bible warns us about those things that can break friendships:

> '...a whisperer separates the best of friends' (Proverbs 16:28) and
> '...he who repeats a matter separates friends' (Proverbs 17:9)

Your best friend may be privileged to know some intimate details about your life, but if he or she shared those secrets with another acquaintance, you would feel completely betrayed. Likewise, when one friend begins to entertain or meditate on the negative words of a third party, that small seed of doubt can begin to form a wedge in the relationship.

Guard your most precious relationships the same way you would guard your heart. Never take them for granted and be careful that you don't overstep the parameters.

Friendship is not a trivial relationship but adds to the fullness of a blessed life. I like the way Charles Swindoll said it: 'Let's face it, friends make life a lot more fun.'

THE POWER OF PARTNERSHIP

'Two *are* better than one,
Because they have a good reward for their labor.
For if they fall, one will lift up his companion.
But woe to him *who is* alone when he falls,
For *he has* no one to help him up.
Again, if two lie down together, they will keep warm;
But how can one be warm *alone?*
Though one may be overpowered by another,
two can withstand him.
And a threefold cord is not quickly broken.'
(Ecclesiastes 4:9-12)

Two are Better than One
'Two *are* better than one...' (Ecclesiastes 4:9)

Don't be fooled into thinking that you have the capacity to achieve your best on your own. A training partner in the gym is a great asset because when you think you have reached your limit, there is someone who can push you to go further.

Having someone who believes in you and encourages you to reach for your dream will add to your life and be a friend to your destiny. It was the blind and deaf Helen Keller who said, 'Alone we can do so little; together we can do so much.' The Bible puts it this way: 'Two *are* better than one...' (Ecclesaistes 4:9)

This verse goes on to list the benefits of partnership and the blessings of intimacy. The desire to have intimate relationships is deep within every human being – be it with our life's partner, our family or close friendships.

To be 'intimate' means to be closely acquainted and familiar with someone else, and within the right parameters, intimacy is one of life's great blessings. Yet to some, intimacy can become a curse. People who carry the scars of painful relationships can allow their past experiences to keep sabotaging their present and future relationships. To protect themselves, some put up walls to prevent others becoming too close to them. Others habitually form intimate relationships with the wrong people for the wrong reasons. To them, intimacy means confusion and pain.

Instead, intimacy should enhance and bless lives. If you have been hurt or betrayed by someone, don't allow that to prevent you from building good relationships in the future. A good starting point is becoming part of a local church that inspires you to expand and grow, building relationships with others whose lives are based on Bible principles.

Greater Impact and Support

'...they have a good reward for their labor.' (Ecclesiastes 4:9)

You have probably heard the saying, 'Many hands make light work.' This implies that teamwork gets a job done faster than one person can. The Bible puts it this way: 'Two are better than one, because they have a good reward for their labor.' (Ecclesiastes 4:9)

Working together enables you to have a greater impact and higher productivity. If you single-handedly tackle a task, such as building a brick wall, it will take considerably longer than two people working together. The reward for the work of two is far greater.

For example, the world's great airlines have formed alliances for the greater benefit of all involved. The reward of good partnerships and relationships is that they make us more effective and fruitful.

'Be fruitful and multiply' was the first command God gave to humanity. Being fruitful and multiplying isn't only about a man and a woman being physically intimate with each other and conceiving children. His will for our lives is that we increase and expand in everything we do. For instance, when we work together in unity, we can achieve so much more and have a greater influence and impact.

Besides achieving more together, two are better than one because you have assistance and support when you need it.

> 'For if they fall, one will lift up his companion.
> But woe to him *who is* alone when he falls,
> For *he has* no one to help him up.' (Ecclesiastes 4:10)

Your intimate friendships and relationships are the ones that will carry you through the hard times and celebrate the good times with you. When you face tough situations in life, those closest to you are the ones who support you by lifting you up when you are down.

Companionship and Strength

'Though one may be overpowered by another,
two can withstand him...' (Ecclesiastes 4:12)

'Two are better than one' is not only a principle that gives you greater impact and support, but also gives you the warmth of companionship and added strength when you are vulnerable.

'Again, if two lie down together, they will keep warm;
But how can one be warm *alone?*' (Ecclesiastes 4:11)

The warmth of a loving, close relationship is one of life's great blessings. It means having someone who rejoices with you when you have reason to celebrate, and who weeps with you when you are in pain. Such intimate relationships add warmth to your life.

Many mistakenly think that sex will produce the intimacy they crave, but outside God's parameters, sex can cause hurt and pain. Many extra-marital affairs aren't as much about lust as they are about the desire to fill that cold, empty void that comes from a lack of intimacy. The power of two also provides strength and protection.

'Though one may be overpowered by another, two can withstand him.' (Ecclesiastes 4:12)

When you stand alone, you are more likely to be overpowered, but when people stand together, it is a much more powerful force. A breakdown in a marriage, a friendship or a team is often started by a wedge provided by a third party who introduces a small seed of doubt. Entertaining thoughts such as imagining you should be somewhere else or with another partner could take you down a path that leads to devastation.

Always remember that the devil's desire is to see strong relationships fail and if he can put a wedge into those partnerships, he will. Yet, in relationships that know genuine closeness and intimacy, any opening for interference by any other third party is firmly closed.

A Threefold Cord

'And a threefold cord is not quickly broken.' (Ecclesiastes 4:12)

During the Second World War, various nations formed an alliance against Nazi Germany. Their common enemy was the reason for the alliance. Whether it is a common goal, a shared vision or cause, or even a common enemy, every relationship has a third factor that binds them together. The Bible states: 'And a threefold cord is not quickly broken.' (Ecclesiastes 4:12)

Every partnership has three strands – firstly, there is you; secondly, there are those you are in partnership with, and the third part of the equation is the common interest that holds relationships together. It is this third cord that determines the impact of the partnership. If you examine the various relationships in your life, you should be able to identify what holds them together. The uniting force of this third element is therefore very important because it determines whether that relationship will be healthy or unhealthy.

The things that unite people are diverse, and can be positive or negative. Bitterness and negativity can bring people together with destructive consequences.

'...Pilate and Herod became friends with each other, for previously they had been at enmity with each other.' (Luke 23:12)

This verse describes two men who previously disliked each other but a shared contempt for Jesus became the third cord that tied their relationship together. When individuals leave a church, a sports club or workplace with a negative or critical spirit, they invariably find others who have shared a similar experience. Their similar attitude or mutual hurt becomes the cord that brings them together.

The most powerful cord is love. The Bible says that love never fails. When love is the primary force that binds a relationship together, there may be challenges, but the partnership will not be broken. The key to great relationships is to build the right third cord into partnerships that will prove indestructible.

Partnering for Success

'...*that* you be perfectly joined together in the same mind
and in the same judgement.' (1 Corinthians 1:10)

Have you ever watched a couple on the dance floor who know how to move exceptionally well together? They blend into one with perfect rhythm and symmetry, and are irresistible to watch.

That is how God intends our partnerships and relationships to be. The Apostle Paul taught about unity and partnership, saying:

> '...that you all speak the same thing, and *that* there be no divisions among you, but *that* you be perfectly joined together in the same mind and in the same judgement.' (1 Corinthians 1:10)

A partnership is an alliance or unified force, with a shared purpose or a common interest. Partners in business share the risk, the costs, the consequences and ultimately share the profits. In a healthy marriage, partners share the bed, share their dreams, and share the blessing or assets of that marriage.

I believe there are things in your life that either attract or repel partnership. Many want the benefits, but aspects of their thinking, their personality or their lifestyle hold them back from building strong relationships.

There are those who were once in a partnership, perhaps a business or marriage relationship, that had disastrous results. They won't allow themselves to get involved again because of the pain and conflict they experienced.

Some think about partnership in selfish terms: 'Oh no, everything I have, I have to split in two!' But in successful partnerships, the rewards are multiplied. If you understand the power of genuinely sharing, it won't restrict you or mean that you have less. It will greatly enhance your life.

Shared Contribution

'...joined and knit together by what every joint
supplies, according to the effective working by which
every part does its share...' (Ephesians 4:16)

A great relationship or partnership is like a two-way street – it involves shared contribution. To enjoy the blessing of partnership you have to put something in to get something out. Today we live in an instant society, where many want the immediate benefits, but they are not prepared for the hard work or cost to get there. They don't want to contribute or give anything, they only want to receive.

There are married couples who never experience the power of partnership. Perhaps they don't understand the importance of being open and transparent with their spouse, so they make little intimate or emotional contribution to their relationship. **Consequently they don't enjoy the** blessing of partnership that God intends. It requires both parties to contribute to a relationship in order for it to succeed.

Similarly, you may attend a local church on a regular basis, but the blessing you experience will be determined by the level of your contribution and partnership in the vision. Those who are sacrificial in their contribution are those who take on the spirit of partnership and enjoy its full blessing.

Even those in leadership positions can miss the power of partnership. If they are insecure or threatened by others, they never see their team as partners and under-estimate their contribution. It is possible to have a large complement of staff who work for you or are around you, but fail to understand what it means to partner in the vision.

What is it like to have a team who does partner with you? If you want to know the blessing of partnership, you need to open yourself up and make your contribution into the lives of others.

Shared Equality

'For *I do* not mean that others should be eased and you burdened;
but by an equality...' (2 Corinthians 8:13-14)

We are all equal in the eyes of God. He made us unique with different roles to fulfil, but that doesn't mean one is superior to another. Unfortunately there are those who distort what the Bible says about submission and so pervert the truth concerning Godly marriage and Godly leadership. They build their relationships on domination or control, and miss the real blessing of partnership that God intended.

Even though leadership will emerge in every relationship, Godly partnerships will enjoy equality. The Apostle Paul wrote:

'For *I do* not mean that others should be eased and you burdened;
but by an equality, *that* now at this time your abundance *may supply* their lack, that their abundance also may *supply* your lack—that there may be equality.' (2 Corinthians 8:13-14)

Great partnerships are based on each one doing their share. In business, it is an unhealthy partnership if one person takes all the risk and the other person enjoys all the profit. Neither will a marriage be healthy if each one sees it in terms of their own interests. 'For richer, for poorer' doesn't mean you get richer and your partner gets poorer. Likewise, 'for better, for worse' doesn't mean better for you and worse for your partner.

Genuine equality understands what it means to be a blessing and brings a desire to empower your partner. If all you are interested in is how things affect you, you cannot experience the true spirit of partnership. A great partner recognises the risk and the cost, and is committed to carrying the share of the load... and ultimately enjoys the shared blessing or reward.

Shared Commitment
'For wherever you go, I will go;' (Ruth 1:16)

Faithfulness and commitment are two more ingredients for a great partnership. There is a Proverb that says:

'Most men will proclaim each his own goodness,
But who can find a faithful man?' (Proverbs 20:6)

The distinction is made between faithfulness and self-interest. The majority of people look out for their own interests, but a faithful person will have a sense of commitment that goes well beyond themself.

Sadly, many are focused on their personal interests rather than putting the combined interests of the partnership first. Don't build your relationships according to the spirit of 'most men' – the attitude of the majority.

In the Old Testament, Ruth displayed an incredible spirit of commitment to her mother-in-law after they both lost their husbands. Instead of abandoning Naomi, this is what Ruth said:

'For wherever you go, I will go; And wherever you lodge, I will lodge; Your people *shall* be my people, and your God, my God. Where you die, I will die, and there will I be buried. The LORD do so to me, and more also, if *anything but* death parts you and me.' (Ruth 1:16-17)

'Until death us do part' is a powerful commitment. Marriage partners may declare this in their wedding vows, but some never live at this level of commitment. There may be things your partner enjoys that you don't, but why not do them willingly and allow their happiness to be your reward?

True commitment involves faithfulness towards the interests of your partner. Such commitment is the hallmark of a great partnership.

Shared Purpose

'...but according to His own purpose...' (2 Timothy 1:9)

Ultimately, partnership is all about a shared purpose. When Hillsong Church made plans to build a new church building, there was a tremendous sense of rallying together as our congregation united to raise the finance. It was the shared purpose and committed partnership to the vision that enabled us to build our new facility.

It is often a sense of purpose or a cause that unites people in the first place. In business partnerships, the shared purpose may be profits. In a marriage, it could be the shared goals of building a family and a home.

Take a young couple who have a vision of building their own home and invest all their time and energy into their goal. They will see the reward of their labours but sadly, that shared purpose (third cord) can sometimes become the destructive element in their relationship. When the house is complete, they could discover there is nothing else between them when their common purpose is gone. Instead of sowing into their relationship, they invested too much into achieving their common goal.

In my book *For This I Was Born* I wrote about the power of partnering for the Cause of the King and the Kingdom. The Bible says: '...God, who has saved us and called *us* with a holy calling, not according to our works, but according to His own purpose...' (2 Timothy 1:8-9)

We are all alive for a specific purpose and a cause, and God will place other people in your life to help you achieve it. You will usually find people are drawn to those who have a sense of purpose. When you lose your sense of purpose, you tend to lose your sense of partnership as well.

It makes sense to examine the cords that are tying your partnerships together to see whether they will ultimately bring fulfilment or failure. Vision brings unity and unity brings reward.

THE POWER OF MARRIAGE

'Then the rib which the LORD God had taken from man He made into a woman, and He brought her to the man.

And Adam said:
"This *is* now bone of my bones
And flesh of my flesh;
She shall be called Woman,
Because she was taken out of Man."

Therefore a man shall leave his father and mother and be joined to his wife, and they shall become one flesh.' (Genesis 2:22-24)

The Blessing of Marriage

'...and they shall become one...' (Genesis 2:24)

I first met my wife Bobbie before her seventeenth birthday, and it was the beginning of a great God-ordained partnership that has enriched every area of my life. We've now been married for many years and I can honestly testify that our marriage is stronger than ever. Is this a fluke? Are we just lucky? The truth is that choices have been made and the effort has been put into building a strong partnership.

'*He who* finds a wife finds a good *thing*' (Proverbs 18:22)

Marriage is God's idea and He purposed it for good. It is the most intimate relationship you will have with another person because it is a powerful spiritual and physical union where two become one.

'Therefore a man shall leave his father and mother and be joined to his wife, and they shall become one flesh.' (Genesis 2:24)

Being joined together describes being attached and connected. It literally means to stick like glue. Try to pull it apart and both parties will experience a lot of hurt and pain. At the culmination of the marriage vows, the minister usually declares the words of Jesus over a couple: 'Therefore what God has joined together, let no man separate.' (Mark 10:9)

The fact is that you never want to pull apart what God has joined together, be it a marriage, or any other God-ordained partnership. On the other hand, you don't want to attempt to put together something that God never intended. Sadly, some people try and join things together that have no future, while others try to pull something apart that is very much part of God's plan.

One of the most significant choices we can ever make relates to the choice of our life partner, so we need to understand what it truly means to be joined together.

Making Right Choices

'Do not be unequally yoked together with
unbelievers.' (2 Corinthians 6:14)

Choosing your marriage partner is one of the most important decisions
you will ever make. Marriage is intended to be the greatest partnership in
life, but when built on a poor foundation, it is doomed to struggle or fail.

There are several reasons why people choose the wrong partner – it can
be a strong physical attraction, becoming involved on the rebound, or
wanting to avoid being single at any cost. Ultimately, they ignore wise
counsel and the warning signals. You can avoid making a serious mistake
by considering these three key warning signs.

• **Watch out for spiritual compatibility** – the Bible is clear that we
should not be unequally yoked. When two lives are pulling in different
directions, something has to give. There will obviously be a potential
source of disagreement and such conflict won't help build a harmonious
marriage. Sharing the same values, morals, ethics and spiritual beliefs is
vital for a blessed partnership.

• **Be careful when there is emotional dysfunction** – Don't ignore
the signs of someone who has a pattern of extreme behaviour. Severe
depression, hypersensitivity or problems such as eating disorders are not
suddenly going to disappear after you get married. We all have issues in life
which need to be overcome but mistakes can be made because of what we
ignore. For example, a cute smile will not mask an ugly temper. A marriage
can be destroyed by emotional problems that haven't been dealt with.

• **Sexual perversion or confusion** – Sex was created to bless a deeply
intimate relationship between husband and wife, but outside God's
parameters, it will only bring hurt and pain. Even when a person has turned
away from their past experiences, it takes time to renew their thinking, and
change old behaviour patterns to line up with the Word.

Both partners will reap what is sown into a marriage, so use Godly wisdom
when it comes to a life-long partnership.

Three Secrets for a Strong Marriage
'Blessed are those whose strength is in you...' (Psalm 84:5 NIV)

From the moment a couple are joined together in marriage, they begin a journey of life together. Like any road travelled, there will inevitably be twists and turns to negotiate. Every marriage has its share of tests and trials, but why do some emerge stronger while others fall apart? I can testify to three key secrets that will help to build a strong marriage.

• Two people who love God
Two people who love God and put Him first in their lives have the ingredient for a strong marriage. When one partner is passionate about God and His purpose but the other isn't, it makes the journey together a lot more difficult.

'Blessed *is* the man whose strength *is* in You...' (Psalm 84:5)

When the strength of your marriage is your commitment to Him, you can go through challenges and emerge stronger.

• Two people who love the House of God
The Bible is clear that one of the keys to a blessed life is our association with God's House (His Church). It says: 'Those who are planted in the house of the LORD shall flourish...' (Psalm 92:13) and, 'Blessed *are* those who dwell in Your house...' (Psalm 84:4)

My personal experience is that the love Bobbie and I share for the Church has been a unifying factor in our marriage and the strength of our family.

• Two people who love each other
It may seem obvious, but the third secret of a blessed marriage is a union of two people who love each other. This is the love that Paul wrote about in 1 Corinthians 13 – it suffers long, it is kind, and it does not envy or parade itself. This love doesn't seek its own, is not provoked and thinks no evil. It bears all things, believes all things, hopes all things and endures all things. This is a love that will 'never fail.'

Building Your Marriage Day-to-Day

'...do not let the sun go down on your wrath...' (Ephesians 4:26)

When a couple admits their marriage is in trouble, it is often the little everyday issues that have been suppressed for a long period of time that create most of the problems. The Bible gives us what may appear to be simple counsel, yet which can prevent these issues from sabotaging your future.

• Resolve issues quickly

'...do not let the sun go down on your wrath...' (Ephesians 4:26) People allow the sun to go down on unforgiveness, resentment, hurt and regret. They carry around baggage from the past that eventually begins to rule their lives. Eventually, all their pent-up anger and their unresolved emotion pours out. Often they have left it until their relationship is irreparable.

The best advice is to deal with issues so that yesterday's pain is not determining the health of your marriage today. Jesus said, 'Sufficient for the day is its own trouble' but many cannot even confront today's challenges because of the junk still occupying them from the past.

• Speak words of life

'Death and life *are* in the power of the tongue,
And those who love it will eat its fruit.' (Proverbs 18:21)

Words bear fruit, positively or negatively – they can either build others up or be lethal weapons of devastation and damage. Whether spoken by you or over you, words have the power to affect your relationships. Thoughtless, careless words can mortally wound a marriage or scar a child for life.

Your words are like deposits in others that can ultimately shape their lives. Encouraging words of praise build confidence and self-worth, but constant criticism and disapproval produces a sense of failure and rejection. The Bible says, 'The lips of the righteous feed many' (Proverbs 10:21). Make a decision to speak words of life that will bless your partner and build them up.

Committed to Your Partner's Success

'...but whoever desires to become great among you,
let him be your servant.' (Matthew 20:26)

When Bobbie and I married, we had both lived in a relatively small world in New Zealand. Over the years I have enjoyed seeing her life grow and expand. Today she has increased in confidence and her gifts and talents have flourished. She has written books and speaks all over the world.

Sadly, there are those who keep their partner suppressed and shackled. Some even use scriptures out of context to control their spouse and keep their world small. Because of this insecurity, their home is full of resentment, hurt and negativity. The truth is that by holding your partner back, you also hold your own life back.

Learn to invest into your partner. Empowering them to become a bigger person will lead to greater horizons for you both. Most Christians recognise Proverbs 31 as depicting the awesome qualities of a Godly woman, but I think you also gain valuable insight into her marriage.

'She makes tapestry for herself;
Her clothing *is* fine linen and purple.
Her husband is known in the gates,
When he sits among the elders of the land.' (Proverbs 31:22-23)

This verse describes a man who is a well-known and influential leader whose wife is obviously able to dress in fine garments. But here is another way of looking at it – perhaps his commitment to dressing his wife in fine linen contributed towards his success.

I'm not talking about the expense of clothes or what people wear, but an attitude that loves blessing and empowering the people around you. If you can see beyond yourself and be committed to seeing your partner flourish, it can open you up to a much bigger, expansive life and build a wonderful marriage.

THE POWER OF FAMILY

'Our Father in Heaven,
Hallowed be Your name.
Your kingdom come.
Your will be done
On earth as *it is* in Heaven.
Give us this day our daily bread.
And forgive us our debts,
As we forgive our debtors.
And do not lead us into
temptation,
But deliver us from the evil one.
For Yours is the kingdom and
the power and the glory forever.
Amen.'
(Matthew 6:9-13)

The Blessing of Children

'...children *are* a heritage from the LORD...' (Psalm 127:3)

I will never forget the day I became a father for the first time. I ran towards my car in the parking lot of St Margaret's hospital in Sydney with an incredible sense of elation. I had a son – I was a dad!

I'll also never forget the second time I became a father – or the third time – because words cannot describe the wonderful experience of becoming a parent. It changes your perspective on life forever. Suddenly the concept of 'family' takes on a whole new meaning.

Someone once said that the family you come from isn't as important as the family you are going to have. When you were born, you were part of someone else's family, but when you become a parent, you create a new family – and with that comes the responsibility of looking after them.

Family, like marriage, is God's idea. The Bible says: '...children *are* a heritage from the LORD.' (Psalm 127:3)

What an incredible gift we are entrusted with – the lives of a new generation. There is no parent on the entire planet who has never made a mistake in their parenting. There is also no sane parent who looked at a newborn child and deliberately intended to mess their life up. The great thing is that the Bible contains a wealth of wisdom and counsel that equips us to raise our children to live life successfully.

Jesus said that our Father in Heaven knows the things we have need of before we ask Him (Matthew 6:8). As parents, our challenge is to know the needs of our children and invest the right ingredients into building their lives.

Giving Your Children Your Best

'Our Father in Heaven, hallowed be Your name. Your kingdom come.
Your will be done on earth as *it is* in heaven.' (Matthew 6:9-10)

The Lord's Prayer is a wonderful example of the Son communicating with
His Father and within this prayer, I have discovered some wonderful advice
about what I can give my children.

• A good name
'Our Father in Heaven, hallowed be Your name...' (Matthew 6:9)
My wife chose to adopt my name when we got married but our children
inherited my name when they were born. A name is something they should
be able to wear with honour, not a liability that brings shame. Give your
children a name with which they can hold their heads high.

• A relationship with God
'Your will be done on earth as *it is* in heaven...' (Matthew 6:10) Children
will always bring you down to earth, so it is important to be relatable
and allow them to be real. Some parents try and take earth to Heaven by
demanding that their children be little angels. Instead we need to take the
things of Heaven and apply them to earth, allowing our children to see the
testimony of God working in our lives. Train them in the ways of God in
a relatable manner that equips them to love God and love life. Help them
to see that the will of God is exciting and can be applied to the real world.

• Being a breadwinner
'Give us this day our daily bread.' (Matthew 6:11) My kids certainly know
where to come when they need money... and I don't mind that. Yet being
the breadwinner is far more than simply providing for the family's material
needs. It includes the responsibility to teach them to tap into the resource of
Heaven for themselves, and to equip them with the wisdom, understanding
and knowledge to live resourcefully, and to know the benefits of hard work,
consistency and generosity.

Your Relationship with Your Children

'And do not lead us into temptation, but deliver us
from the evil one.' (Matthew 6:13)

God as a father gives us a pattern for the kind of relationship we can build
with our children that will positively influence their lives.

• Be a friend

'...forgive us our debts, as we forgive our debtors.' (Matthew 6:12) One of
the great challenges is not only to be a parent, but also to be a friend to your
children. Some parents never give their children room to grow and never
forgive them for their shortcomings. Instead of forcing them to become
what you want them to be, accept them for who they are and let them be
who they are destined to be.

• Be a leader

'...do not lead us into temptation.' (Matthew 6:13) Where are you leading
your children? Is your example leading your children into temptation to
rebel in life? Leadership is about example, and the example you set is the
example they will follow. You cannot successfully be a parent who says,
'Do what I say but not what I do.'

• Be a coach or trainer

'...deliver us from the evil one.' (Matthew 6:13) A good coach is one who
encourages sports players in their strengths and helps them to overcome
their weaknesses in order to be successful.

As parents, we have the opportunity to shape the lives of our children and
equip them with positive life skills. Sadly, there are those who haven't been
coached to live life well. Perhaps you were raised by an austere parent who
was always critical and didn't know how to give or receive love. Yet we
can deliver our children from the clutches of poor examples of the past
and coach them to be overcomers through exemplifying the way they
should go. The way we think is passed down through generations and our
responsibility is to train up our children to live a blessed life.

Training Children Up

'Train up a child in the way he should go, and when he is old
he will not depart from it.' (Proverbs 22:6)

The Bible says that if you train up children in the way they should go, they will not depart from it when they are old. The flipside of that scripture applies as well. If you train up children in the way they shouldn't go, they will not easily depart from that way either.

For instance, you may have grown up with a battler or struggler's mentality and are unable to comprehend any other way of living except by struggling financially. That's the way your parents thought and so you were trained to think that way too. Today there is a trend to target parents as the source of blame for your own failures in life. While it may be necessary to identify where your behaviour originated, this is no excuse or reason to stay that way.

No matter what your upbringing was, you can change the future generations by becoming a wise parent to your children. The Bible contains some excellent keys for investing into the lives of children and training them up in the way they should go.

• Godly discipline
'Discipline your children, and they will give you peace; they will bring delights you desire.' (Proverbs 29:17 NIV) The key to discipline is consistency, rather than lashing out when you lose your temper. If you are consistent about what you do and say, you will raise great children.

• Love them, but don't spoil them
'If a man pampers his servant from youth, he will bring grief in the end.' (Proverbs 29:21 NIV) There is a vast difference between loving and spoiling your children. Remember that love will include chastening your child when need be. Every child needs to know that every action has a consequence (or as the Bible puts it – we reap what we sow).

Investing into Your Children

'Where there is no vision, the people perish...' (Proverbs 29:18 KJV)

Children who grow up hearing 'You're hopeless' or 'You'll never amount to anything' inevitably tend to believe it. The words you speak are powerful, and what you say will influence and impact the lives of your children.

• Live by Godly principles

'...blessed is he who keeps the law.' (Proverbs 29:18 NIV) Previously I mentioned the importance of setting an example for your children to follow and to train them up in the way they should go. Living by Bible principles means you will see Bible results. Telling your children that they should 'honour their father and mother' is more powerful when they see how you honour your parents.

• Fill their lives with vision

'Where there is no vision, the people cast off restraint;' (Proverbs 29:18 ASV) You cannot ignore the link between rebellion and lack of a vision. Without purpose, there is a sense of hopelessness and people begin to live carelessly. Encourage your children to reach for their dreams and you will give them direction and purpose in life.

• Take responsibility for a peaceful home

'An angry man stirs up dissension, and a hot-tempered one commits many sins.' (Proverbs 29:22 NIV) Take responsibility for creating the atmosphere of your home. Peace is often the same word used for 'prosperity' in the Bible, and by keeping an even temper, your family will enjoy the blessing of a happy home.

• Be humble

'A man's pride brings him low, but a man of lowly spirit gains honor.' (Proverbs 29:23 NIV) Have you ever said 'sorry' to your children? Pride will always bring devastation, and many families have been devastated by the inability of parents to confront their own mistakes. Transparency and honesty are invaluable.

Building Great Relationships

'Love suffers long *and* is kind; love does not envy; love does not parade itself, is not puffed up; does not behave rudely, does not seek its own; is not provoked, thinks no evil; does not rejoice in iniquity, but rejoices in the truth; bears all things, believes all things, hopes all things, endures all things. Love never fails.' (1 Corinthians 13:4-8)

Priorities for Great Relationships

'But seek first the kingdom of God and His righteousness,
and all these things shall be added to you.' (Matthew 6:33)

A great marriage and family, as well as friendships and partnerships, are built on putting them first in your life. Give them second place and you will have second-rate relationships.

The reality is, if you want great relationships, you will need to make them a priority. Jesus teaches us three priorities for our relationships – the things that should come first.

• 'First be reconciled to your brother...' (Matthew 5:24)
If you have a fallout in a close intimate relationship, it is important to work towards reconciliation. Holding on to bitterness and anger can rule and impact every aspect of your life. The Bible instructs us to 'pursue peace' (Hebrews 12:14) so whether it is with family, a work colleague or a friend, get your relationships in order. Some destructive relationships need to be severed completely, but settle them quickly and move on.

• 'First remove the plank from your own eye...' (Matthew 7:5)
Human nature tends to see what is wrong with others more easily than seeing what needs changing within oneself. Instead of being judgemental and critical, learn to live with a positive, encouraging spirit towards others. Don't be harsh in your thinking but rather believe the best in people. Why not give them the benefit of the doubt?

• '...sit down first and count the cost...' (Luke 14:28)
Jesus taught us how to count the cost before we begin anything. As a friend, how far will you go to help someone in need? As a partner, are you prepared to ride the challenges that come your way? As a parent, can you love your children no matter what they do?

There will always be obstacles to face in all your relationships, but if you have evaluated the cost beforehand, you can go the distance.

Your Relationship with God

'...that I may know Him...' (Philippians 3:10)

It is impossible to write a book on building great relationships without mentioning the most important relationship of all – your relationship with God. Many people *know about* God, but they miss the blessing of *knowing Him* personally. Some never know that they can. Sadly, many spend their lives running from Him, not realising that they can have a personal relationship with the One who is committed to seeing them succeed in every area of life.

Your relationship with God has the power to impact every other relationship you have. Once you know Him, every other relationship has the added potential to be a success and a blessing.

God created us to know the blessing of intimacy – to have close fellowship and a personal relationship with Him. It was never His intention to have robotic creatures that He could control from Heaven, like puppets on a string.

The original intentions of God for mankind are described in the book of Genesis. Not only did He give Adam and Eve everything they could ever want or need, but they had an intimate relationship with Him, walking and talking with Him in the perfection of creation. It was only after they disregarded God's command not to eat from the tree of good and evil that they hid from Him, and sin caused the great rift in the relationship between God and humanity.

This is where the awesome unconditional love God has for us is revealed. Whereas man was responsible for breaking the relationship with God, God took responsibility for restoring His relationship with man. He sent His most precious possession – His Son, Jesus – to bring reconciliation. That's the Gospel in a nutshell – acknowledging who Jesus is and what He did enables every one of us to have that wonderful, intimate relationship with God again.

Epilogue: Friends Family Faith

Bobbie and I have now been married for over thirty-five years, surrounded by the wonderful family and friends God has placed in our lives. The glory of that milestone in our journey goes to God.

Psalm 84 describes the blessing of God on those whose strength is in Him, 'whose hearts are set on pilgrimage' (Psalm 84:5 NIV). Our marriage, family and friendships have all been set on the journey we travel together in faith, committed to the Cause of Christ.

The words 'Friends Family Faith' used to adorn the wall of our church reception foyer. These words encapsulate the healthy relationships that contribute to the healthy, functional church we are today. Essentially, we are all part of a very big family – the family of God. The Bible says: 'God sets the solitary in families' (Psalm 68:6)

One of the signs of a blessed life is healthy relationships and the Word of God gives us the principles we need to build them. When you recognise that the Bible contains the keys to building great relationships across the spectrum of your life, you will begin to tap into the blessing God has for you.

One cannot put a value on great relationships. They don't come by chance but sowing or investing into others will reap the highest rewards.

May all your relationships go from strength to strength.
Brian Houston

BOOK THREE

HOW TO FLOURISH IN LIFE

PRINCIPLES FOR BUILDING A
THRIVING, PRODUCTIVE LIFE

HOW TO MAXIMISE YOUR LIFE

God's People Should Flourish

I have two great passions: one is to build the Church of Jesus Christ, and the other is to help God's people fulfil their potential in life. The fact is that both of these are inter-related and each one supports the other. When the Church thrives, God's people are equipped to fulfil their potential, and when God's people flourish, they instinctively build His Church.

One of my favourite scriptures is found in Psalm 92:

> 'Those who are planted in the house of the LORD
> Shall flourish in the courts of our God.
> They shall still bear fruit in old age;
> They shall be fresh and flourishing,' (Psalm 92:13-14)

A revelation of this powerful promise of God can change your life and produce wonderful results across the span of your life. When you decide to plant yourself in God's House, you will thrive. Not only can I testify to this in my own life, but that of my family, my ministry colleagues and our church congregation. The fruit is evident for all to see.

We all face challenges and obstacles at various times, but God's will is for you to flourish and succeed in every area of your life – from your relationships to your career, in your health and finances, to your spiritual life and your church.

The Bible is full of promise and encouragement to this end and there is no reason why you should settle for anything less than God's best. The wonderful thing is that He has set you up to flourish in life because He has deposited seeds of the highest potential within you. No matter what you are facing right now or where you are positioned, God has so much more in store for you.

I pray that in the following pages, you will receive some great insights into how you can live at the highest level of life purposed for you, because you were created and destined to flourish and go from strength to strength.

Why Should You Flourish?

'Those who are planted in the house of the LORD
Shall flourish in the courts of our God.' (Psalm 92:13)

There is nothing I like better than to see God's people expanding and increasing in every area of their lives. I believe you are alive to make a difference, and an increased life empowers you to impact and influence others in a positive way.

There are some who would argue against the need for Christians to be prosperous or successful, but I present this question: Is it an option for believers to flourish when it is in their hand to do so, or is it a responsibility? In fact, there are three important reasons why God's people should live flourishing lives. Firstly, when we flourish across every aspect of our lives, we are aligning ourselves with the objectives of Jesus. He said: 'I have come that they may have life, and that they may have *it* more abundantly.' (John 10:10)

God's purpose and intention is clearly that we should have an abundant life – that means bountiful, productive, successful, prosperous... and flourishing! This kind of abundant life reveals and demonstrates the power of God to others.

The second reason why I believe it is important for God's people to flourish is that it empowers us to have a greater impact. Our ability to make a difference in the lives of others is limited if we are crippled by debt, sickness or emotional dysfunction. Certainly, our God is a present help for anyone in trouble, but His purpose is to help people to overcome these difficulties so we can be in a position of strength to help others.

Thirdly, I believe if people cannot flourish, they are unlikely to stay planted. The House of the Lord should be an environment where people can flourish and become who God purposed them to be. I don't believe God intended His Church to remain small and contained, but rather to keep expanding and enlarging, giving people an opportunity to reach their potential.

Fresh and Flourishing
'They shall be fresh and flourishing...' (Psalm 92:14)

When I first started teaching on the subject of 'God's People Should Flourish,' I began to examine the way Psalm 92 describes those who are planted in the House of the Lord: 'They shall be fresh and flourishing.' In the reference margin of my Bible, the note says that fresh means fat and flourishing means green like a healthy tree.

I had some fun with our congregation at the time, telling them that God's will for them was to be fat and green, and also full of sap (Psalm 104:16 says, 'The trees of the LORD are full of *sap*').

I then went on to tell them that my desire was to build a church of 'fat, green saps'. For a number of weeks these became the buzz words in church life. In fact, one young girl had a bright green T-shirt made for herself, emblazoned with the words, 'FAT AND GREEN!'

While the words literally refer to the qualities of a plant, they also give us a clear picture of what our lives should look like: fat in terms of our lives being successful, expansive and full of Kingdom purpose; green in terms of being healthy, growing and producing fruit.

As a Senior Pastor, I have to ask myself a very important question: 'Can the people in our church flourish under my ministry? And if not, why would they stay planted?' I believe it is necessary for believers to be in a local church that facilitates growth and expansion in their lives. If not, they would be better off finding a place where they can flourish.

Psalm 92 states, 'Those who are planted in the House of the Lord shall flourish in the courts of our God.' It doesn't say, 'Those who *attend* the House of the Lord' but 'those who are *planted* in the House of the Lord.' There is a difference. To be successful and to flourish the way God intended requires you to be planted. Not everyone who attends church will flourish, but the promise is to those who are planted.

Seeds of Potential
'Yet I had planted you a noble vine, a seed of
highest quality...' (Jeremiah 2:21)

It is impossible to plant tomato seeds and reap carrots. Tomato seeds will produce tomatoes; orange seeds will produce oranges. Within each seed is the potential to produce and reproduce a specific kind of fruit.

Have you ever wondered why the Bible uses the term 'the *seed* of Abraham' or 'the *seed* of David'? It does so because the seed of spiritual destiny and potential is carried from generation to generation. **Within every living** thing is deposited a seed with the ability to reproduce itself. This is how God created it to be. The Bible says:

> 'Yet I had planted you a noble vine, a seed of highest quality.
> How then have you turned before Me
> Into the degenerate plant of an alien vine?' (Jeremiah 2:21)

These words describe how He has deposited within each of us seeds of the highest quality and calibre, which are purposed to grow into a 'noble vine'. These are the seeds of great potential which enable us to succeed and thrive in every area of life, including business, ministry, relationships and health.

Yet in spite of the reality that these seeds of excellence and distinction are planted within everyone, so many people can tragically become degenerate or inferior versions of what God intends them to be. An 'alien vine' is how the scripture describes it.

So what does it take for a seed of the highest quality to become the fat, green noble vine that God intends it to be? There are three basic requirements for a plant to thrive. Firstly, it needs to be planted in *good soil*; secondly, it needs to be *watered or nourished regularly*; and thirdly, the *environment* surrounding it determines how well it will flourish.

Psalm 92 gives a wonderful analogy of a seed planted in fertile soil. It thrives and bears fruit – this is what our lives should look like too.

Degenerate Plant or Noble Vine?

'How then have you turned before me into the degenerate
plant of an alien vine?' (Jeremiah 2:21)

So if God has placed seeds of the highest quality within us, why is it that so many lives fall short of His finest? How is it possible for a seed of the highest quality to become an alien vine? This verse in Jeremiah reveals the reason:

> 'Your own wickedness will correct you,
> And your backslidings will rebuke you.
> Know therefore and see that *it is* an evil and bitter *thing*
> That you have forsaken the LORD your God...' (Jeremiah 2:19)

Israel was destined to inherit God's blessing and promise, but they began to backslide from God. To backslide literally means to lose all forward momentum. The moment you stop moving forward in Christ is the moment you stop growing, and other things (alien to God's heart for you) begin to flourish instead of His purposes.

In some churches, for example, a vine of negativity, disunity and even carnality flourishes, instead of a vine of encouragement, unity and true spirituality. You may know people who were once actively involved in their local church but gradually began to fall away from serving God. The seeds of the highest quality which began to flourish became withered and stunted. Instead of emerging into a noble vine, they became an 'alien vine' – alien to the purposes of God. The Bible describes such people in this way:

> 'They are like stunted shrubs in the desert,
> with no hope for the future.' (Jeremiah 17:6 NLT)

This paints a bleak picture of someone who was once growing but now stands paralysed in a dry desert wasteland–purposeless and hopeless. Within them a seed of the highest quality still remains, and often all it takes is some good fertile soil and regular nourishment to revive it. Remember, where there is life, there is hope!

Planted in the Right Place

'Behold, *it is* planted, will it thrive? Will it not utterly wither
when the east wind touches it?' (Ezekiel 17:10)

I am committed to building a healthy church where people are nourished
so they can flourish and grow as God intended. As already stated, the
promise of a flourishing life is not for those who *attend* church but those
who are *planted* in His House. Being planted means you allow your roots
to go deep.

When you buy a particular tree or shrub from a nursery, it usually comes
with a label describing the ideal conditions for it to flourish. Some do
better in full sun, and others in shady, damp conditions. The key is to plant
it correctly. The fact is that many people are also planted incorrectly and
the fruit of their lives proves the reality of this point.

The Bible asks this question: 'Behold, *it is* planted, will it thrive? Will it not
utterly wither when the east wind touches it? It will wither in the garden
terrace where it grew.' (Ezekiel 17:10)

You may be planted but can you thrive? If you are planted exactly where
God has purposed you to be, the conditions should be favourable for
successful growth. Psalm 1 is a great illustration of a flourishing life and
carries a promise for those planted in a life-giving location.

'He shall be like a tree
Planted by the rivers of water,
That brings forth its fruit in its season,
Whose leaf also shall not wither;
And whatever he does shall prosper.' (Psalm 1:3)

When you are planted in the right place and in an environment designed to
shape your 'seeds of the highest quality', you will produce fruit in the right
or perfect season, you will grow stronger and taller, and you will flourish
and prosper in every area of life.

Appearance, Behaviour and Fruit

'He shall be like a tree planted by the rivers of water,
that brings forth its fruit in its season...' (Psalm 1:3)

Nature study experiments at school have had many of us planting seeds in dusty soil or even moistened cotton wool. The object of the lesson was to *look* for signs of growth. Those seeds may have begun well but most would end up as degenerate, alien plants.

There are three specific tell-tale signs that reveal whether or not someone is truly flourishing or not.

One of the first signs of health is *appearance*. A flourishing plant is attractive and pleasant to look at because of its lovely fresh foliage. Likewise, the countenance of those who are flourishing will be radiant and shine with His joy. Everyone likes to be around such people, and even in the midst of challenges such people maintain their joy.

You will also recognise those who are flourishing by their *behaviour*. As deciduous and evergreen trees are identified by their behaviour patterns, so believers are identifiable by their behaviour patterns. Some come to church but never enter into worship or participate in the service. Others adopt a cynical or negative attitude about anything and everything. On the other hand, those who are flourishing will lean towards life and worship God with a sense of wholeheartedness. The words on their lips will be positive and uplifting.

Finally, you can identify a flourishing life by its *fruit*. The first instruction God gave humanity was to be fruitful and multiply. If you are bearing fruit, you should be seeing increase and expansion across the spectrum of your life – clear evidence that God is working in your life.

Of course we all need to be mindful of seasons and that time is required to see things come to maturity, but living by God's ways promises that the harvest is guaranteed in our lives.

Cedars of Lebanon

'The righteous shall flourish like a palm tree, he shall
grow like a cedar in Lebanon.' (Psalm 92:12)

The Bible often uses the analogy of trees and plants to illustrate the
spiritual condition of our lives. For example, Psalm 92 says: 'The righteous
shall flourish like a palm tree, He shall grow like a cedar in Lebanon.'
(Psalm 92:12)

The cedars of Lebanon were considered to be among the greatest of all
trees in the ancient world and are frequently mentioned in the Scriptures.
Once plentiful, they are now somewhat rare, but the attributes of this kind
of tree are what God intends for our lives.

Tall and beautiful, the cedars of Lebanon symbolise strength and
magnificence. The fact that they were such colossal trees, growing to over
100 feet tall, meant they required a lot of nourishment, but their purpose
went beyond mere visual splendour. The Bible says:

'The trees of the LORD are full of *sap*,
The cedars of Lebanon which He planted,
Where the birds make their nests;' (Psalm 104:16-17)

The cedars of Lebanon 'which He planted' weren't only impressive to
look at but they served a greater purpose. They produced exceptionally
good wood that was both aromatic and durable. So superior was the
wood that Solomon imported it for the temple in Jerusalem and other
building projects.

This analogy also relates to us. Such people stand tall and strong above
the rest; they are firmly established, resilient and thriving in every area of
life. Such Kingdom-minded people understand they have a purpose far
greater than themselves and are committed to resource the work of God
upon the earth by providing from their substance.

This is a great illustration of a blessed and flourishing life, planted and
nourished by God Himself – a picture of what you are actually destined
to look like.

Flourishing Lives Bear Fruit

'You will know them by their fruits.' (Matthew 7:16)

The very first instruction God gave humanity was simply this, 'Be fruitful and multiply.' (Genesis 1:28)

It isn't actually an option for believers to be fruitful, it is a responsibility that carries consequence. In Mark 11 we read a sobering story. Jesus was hungry so He went over to a fig tree to see if He could find any fruit. All it offered was green leaves, so He cursed it. Obviously we are courting danger by putting on the same facade. The reason for our existence is to build the Kingdom and impact the lives of others.

A person's belief is revealed by their actions, and a church's belief is revealed by what it does. Jesus said: 'And these signs will follow those who believe...' (Mark 16:17)

The fruit of your life doesn't lie. Throughout the Bible, we read of the blessings (or signs) that follow those who live according to God's principles. For instance, success and prosperity are the promise of God in Joshua 1:8. If you keep living by His principles, no matter what comes against you, you are a candidate for success and prosperity.

By appearances, the Pharisees were the most respected religious scholars of the time, but Jesus pointed out the futility of their works because they never produced any fruit that benefitted others. He said:

> 'You will know them by their fruits. Do men gather grapes from thornbushes or figs from thistles? Even so, every good tree bears good fruit, but a bad tree bears bad fruit.' (Matthew 7:16-17)

Whether we like it or not, people will judge us by the fruit of our lives. Sometimes their particular mindset may colour their perception, but do others look at you and see good fruit? A flourishing church creates an environment where good people produce good fruit. I hope you live in such an environment!

Will Your Seed Bear Fruit?
'Unless the Lᴏʀᴅ builds the house, they labor
in vain who build it;' (Psalm 127:1)

How can any of us know that what we are sowing our lives into will prove fruitful and productive on the scale of eternity? Ask yourself the following questions.

• What am I building?
Jesus said He would build His Church, and I believe there is nothing greater we can do than commit to help build what He said He would build.

> '...on this rock I will build My church, and the gates of Hades shall not prevail against it.' (Matthew 16:18)

Sadly, there are those who continually criticise the Church, not realising that instead of building it, they are tearing down something very precious to God.

In this life, we have the opportunity to build so many things – from a marriage and family, to a home and a career, to the testimony or legacy that we will leave behind us. Some people build the wrong things into their lives – they build walls instead of unity in their relationships, or they build a mountain of debt instead of a mountain of resource in their finances. Instead of building a testimony to a life flourishing in God, they are left with a sense of failure and futility. If you want to flourish in life, everything you build should line up with or complement what He is building – His Church.

• What do I love?
Jesus loved His Church and gave Himself for her. If you want to know what someone really loves, watch what they give themselves to. For example, avid gardeners spend their time gardening; musicians give their time to listening to or playing music. Radical followers of Jesus Christ involve themselves in their Father's labour. As Jesus said: 'For where your treasure is, there your heart will be also.' (Matthew 6:21) If you want to flourish in life, love what He loves and give yourself to it.

What are You Adding to?

'But seek first the kingdom of God and His righteousness, and all these things shall be added to you.' (Matthew 6:33)

• What am I adding to?

What are you contributing to on a daily basis? Some add nothing more than humanistic opinions, quarrelsome arguments, or rumours and strife. All they are adding is confusion and chaos, where nothing good can flourish.

'And the Lord added to the church daily those who were being saved.' (Acts 2:47)

A flourishing life will add to or enhance the work of the Lord. There are numerous things you can contribute towards building God's Kingdom, such as a positive attitude, godly thinking, words of life and an unwavering commitment to the House of God. The great and wonderful thing is that as we add to His purposes, God also adds to our lives. Jesus promised: 'But seek first the kingdom of God and His righteousness, and all these things shall be added to you.' (Matthew 6:33)

• What am I confronting?

Here is a thought that many believers prefer to avoid. Jesus was never one to stand back and complacently or helplessly shrug off immature behaviour. He always confronted poor thinking, particularly among the religious leaders of the day.

'Then Jesus went into the temple of God and drove out all those who bought and sold in the temple, and overturned the tables of the money changers and the seats of those who sold doves.' (Matthew 21:12)

In confronting the attitudes of the merchants, Jesus turned things right side up – the way they should be. There are many attitudes and mindsets that need to be confronted and turned right side up in order for the Church to thrive. If you want to flourish, you will need to confront your attitudes and align your thinking to God's purpose for His Church.

What are You Supplying?

'...that you, always having all sufficiency in all *things*, may have
an abundance for every good work.' (2 Corinthians 9:8)

• What am I supplying?

God's plan is for His Church to be a place of provision or, as the Old
Testament refers to it, a *storehouse*. It is a place where people can come and
receive from the abundance of the supply.

The House of God, besides providing a place where you can worship God
and receive the Word, should also be able to provide people with other
things, such as pastoral care, crisis intervention, prayer and meaningful
fellowship. When people have needs, we (the Church) should be in a
position to meet them. Imagine if someone came to the Church for help
and we had to turn them away because we had nothing to give them?

When people are floundering in life, the Church is where they should find
the practical and spiritual sustenance that helps to encourage and restore
them. Paul describes God's plan of supply: 'And God *is* able to make all
grace abound toward you, that you, always having all sufficiency in all
things, may have an abundance for every good work.' (2 Corinthians 9:8)

There are two key concepts relating to supply and provision in this portion
of scripture.

Sufficiency relates to you and your needs. God's plan is that you always
have 'all sufficiency in all things'. Sufficient doesn't mean only enough to get
by on – it means all you need. Paul wrote: 'And my God shall supply all your
need according to His riches in glory by Christ Jesus.' (Philippians 4:19)

Abundance relates to your increased capacity to supply and provide for
the needs of others. God has gone further than ensuring that only your
needs are met, but that 'you have an abundance for every good work.'
His blessing of abundance is not for you to store up for yourself, but His
purpose is to resource you to be an agent of supply.

Building a Flourishing Church

'Beloved, I pray that you may prosper in all things...' (3 John 2)

I honestly love seeing people flourish and increase in life, and I could fill a book with stories of people who have planted themselves in our church and are realising their dreams.

A great example is our previous worship pastor, Darlene Zschech, who has earned world-wide influence and respect in the area of praise and worship. Many see the fruit of her life but aren't fully aware of the passion and devotion with which Darlene and her husband Mark have planted themselves in God's House. For many years they whole-heartedly sowed their lives into building the Kingdom to faithfully carve out a path that has inspired many others. It is no wonder that they are flourishing.

There are many pastors who would love to have Darlene as their worship leader, but could they handle a worship pastor more famous than them? If I was insecure or threatened by the success of any of my team, I would more than likely suppress them. However, I know that I need to build a church that is big enough to fulfil their dreams.

3 John 2 describes how prosperity and health are the results of a prosperous soul. Those who are planted in the House and share the load constitute the healthy soul of a church. Their commitment and contribution causes the local House and greater Body of Christ to flourish. Paul revealed four distinct attitudes or levels of involvement among Christians in his letter to Timothy:

> 'Command those who are rich in this present age not to be haughty, nor to trust in uncertain riches but in the living God, who gives us richly all things to enjoy. *Let them* do good, that they be rich in good works, ready to give, willing to share, storing up for themselves a good foundation for the time to come, that they may lay hold on eternal life.' (1 Timothy 6:17-19)

In the following pages, we'll examine four levels of Christian growth and maturity and how they contribute to and build the Church.

First Level: Enjoyment

The first level of Christianity is enjoyment. Paul wrote to trust 'in the living God, who gives us richly all things to enjoy.' (1 Timothy 6:17)

God has given us so many things to enjoy. Paul warns against trusting in uncertain riches, but the issue is not so much about riches as it is one of trust. God doesn't have a problem with us having things – He has a problem with *things having us*!

There is nothing wrong with Christians enjoying life and having a good sense of humour. Sadly, some believers are far too serious about everything. I've always believed that Christians should be the most magnetic people – the ones everyone wants to hang out with because they are so much fun – the life and soul of any party. I love, for example, the enthusiasm and excitement of new Christians. They are like sponges, eagerly soaking up everything that their new life in Christ has to offer.

The focus of this *first level of Christian growth* is about you and the exciting discovery of what God has in store for your life. For instance, teachings on blessing or success will be about *your* gain; worship will be about *your* personal preference of songs; and friendships will be built around the good times *you* are having.

There are many things God intends for us to enjoy, but enjoyment is not *all* that He has for those who are planted in His House.

It is far better to enjoy church than to endure it, but if our Christianity only extends to enjoyment, we only scratch the surface of God's purposes. There is so much more.

Second Level: Servanthood

The second level of Christianity is servanthood. *'Let them* do good, that they be rich in good works...' (1 Timothy 6:18)

Christians who rise to this second level are those who have added to their enjoyment by committing to serve in God's House. Volunteers such as ushers or helpers who serve others with a willing heart, make a valuable contribution to building the Church on the earth.

Every year our Hillsong Conference draws thousands of delegates from all over the world. The conference always has a great line-up of internationally-recognised speakers and musicians, but we have discovered that the greatest praise on the delegate feedback forms is always reserved for the spirit of the volunteers. Our contingent of volunteers at Hillsong Conference is now well into the thousands, and continues to grow each year. They are the ones who arrive before anyone else in the morning (to set up) and leave well after everyone else in the evenings (after cleaning up). They not only do it selflessly, but they do it cheerfully.

As the Bible instructs us:
'Serve the LORD with gladness;' (Psalm 100:2)

Some Christians serve in God's House, but they do it grudgingly or out of obligation. Somewhere along the line, they lost their enjoyment. While serving is part of 'doing good,' the challenge is to serve with a spirit of gladness.

The key is to still keep enjoying God's House (first level), and apply yourself to serve Him with good works (second level). What is the point of giving your time and not enjoying it?

Third Level: Giving

The third level of Christianity is a revelation of giving. The verse continues... 'ready to give.' (1 Timothy 6:18)

It is wonderful to watch new Christians rise from the level of enjoyment to become actively involved in serving in God's House, and then go on to gain a revelation of what the spirit of giving is all about.

Some people are happy to volunteer or serve, but are much less enthusiastic when challenged to give. They can end up limiting their own lives because they never discover that it really is more blessed to give than to receive. (Acts 20:35)

Whenever a preacher addresses the subject of giving or finance, such people are immediately resistant or defensive. The reality is that people will always rise to defend the thing they love, and sadly, 'the love of money' is an attitude that prevents many from advancing in the purposes of God.

If you want to move to a deeper level of involvement in God's House, you will need to expand in the area of giving. Test yourself. When it is time to receive the tithes and offerings in church, what is your response? Do you come prepared with your tithe and are you excited about giving, or do you react in defence or annoyance?

To move to the third level of Christianity requires a spirit of liberality and a revelation of the words of Jesus: 'Freely you have received, freely give.' (Matthew 10:8)

Fourth Level: Sharing the Load

The fourth level of Christianity is about carrying the load, or as Paul put it, 'willing to share.' (1 Timothy 6:18)

If a malnourished orphan was led on to the platform of a church, most of those observing would be willing to give generously for the provision of the child. But how many would be prepared to take the child home?

Christians who share the load are the ones who will do whatever it takes to fulfil the vision. Religion has developed a concept that clergy is separate from laity, but there is nothing biblical about that belief. A flourishing church involves more people than the senior leadership alone. Paul described the purpose of the five-fold ministry: '...for the equipping of the saints for the work of the ministry, for the edifying of the body of Christ...' (Ephesians 4:12)

Apostles, prophets, evangelists, pastors and teachers are given to inspire and teach everyone involved. The 'work of the ministry' is actually the responsibility of every believer. Church life is comprised of all four types of believers and at the core of a healthy church are those who own the vision and help carry the load of responsibility.

There have been many in our congregation who have sacrificed for many years to finance our new building and today, many new believers are enjoying the benefits of those who were ready to give and willing to share.

Plant yourself in God's House and you will begin to flourish, and as you do, you will keep expanding and moving into new levels of responsibility and growth.

Flourishing Financially

'I will bless you and make your name great;
and you shall be a blessing.' (Genesis 12:2)

Mother Theresa spent her life attending to poverty-stricken people and gathered phenomenal resource to relieve them from that poverty.

People mistakenly believe that Jesus taught against money, but the real issue is that Jesus taught about our *attitude* towards money. The problem isn't money, but our thinking towards it. If there is one subject people really get uptight about, it is the subject of money.

Over the centuries, there has been a lot of upside-down thinking about wealth and finance that has limited the effectiveness of the Church. For too long God's people have been discouraged from flourishing financially and the result has been that they have been limited in their ability to make a huge impact in blessing others.

In Psalm 92, the analogy of the flourishing tree that bears fruit in its season reveals the purpose of God. If fruit remains on the tree, it never blesses or provides for anyone. We are called to be fruitful and multiply in order to fulfil God's purpose on the earth to be a blessing to others. God's purpose for blessing us is revealed in these words:

'I will make you a great nation;
I will bless you
And make your name great;
And you shall be a blessing.' (Genesis 12:2)

The purpose of God's promise to Abraham is clear '...and you shall be a blessing!' The blessing and influence didn't stop with Abraham and his own well-being – it was about being a blessing to others.

Why does God want you to flourish and prosper in life? So you can live well beyond yourself and bless others.

Your Thinking Determines What Thrives
'For as he thinks in his heart, so *is* he.' (Proverbs 23:7)

What you allow to flourish in your thinking has a powerful impact on who you are and what you become. The Bible puts it like this: 'For as he thinks in his heart, so *is* he.' (Proverbs 23:7)

When you allow your heart and thinking to line up with the Word of God, you will begin to become the person He says you are. Sadly, there are Christians who once thrived in the purposes of God, but have now become stunted and stale – all because they indulged in thoughts that should have been weeded out immediately.

Thoughts which are negative, cynical or defeatist are all contrary to the heart of God. So are feelings of bitterness and rejection. Jesus warned us that offences will come, but the danger is in allowing an offence to dominate your thoughts. The Apostle Paul warns us to be diligent: '...lest any root of bitterness springing up cause trouble, and by this many become defiled;' (Hebrews 12:15)

Allow an offence to take root and you may find yourself dealing with a stronghold of bitterness. Paul tells us how to effectively deal with such thoughts:

'... pulling down strongholds, casting down arguments and every high thing that exalts itself against the knowledge of God, bringing every thought into captivity to the obedience of Christ...' (2 Corinthians 10:4-5)

Quickly take negative thoughts, wrong perceptions or offences captive before they take root. Arrest them before they sabotage your life. The progression towards a stronghold always starts with a thought, so it is vital to keep your thinking clean, clear and lined up with God's Word.

Taking Thoughts Captive

'...bringing every thought into captivity to the
obedience of Christ...' (2 Corinthians 10:5)

One thought, unchallenged, can tragically change the course of your life. The progression from the seed of a thought to a flourishing stronghold has four specific stages, according to 2 Corinthians 10:4-5:

1. Thoughts

'...bringing every thought into captivity to the obedience of Christ...' Paul urges us to take every thought captive and line it up with the Word because, if left to roam free, it can become a potential threat to God's purposes. It is easier to pull a weed out of a garden when it is still small so arrest your thoughts in the early stages before they take deep root and become a 'high thing.'

2. High things

'...every high thing that exalts itself against the knowledge of God...' When a thought becomes a 'high thing', it begins to dominate or constantly preoccupy your mind. At night, your mind may race with thoughts or fears that all seem so much bigger than they really are. It is these preoccupying thoughts that cause you to lose perspective as 'high things' elevate themselves above God's Word.

3. Arguments

'...casting down arguments...' Once a thought has become a high thing, it can progress to an argument. No longer is it only in your mind but you could make an argument out of it. Defending such thinking shows that it has started to make sense to you and your perspective has begun to blur.

4. Strongholds

'...pulling down strongholds...' A stronghold is exactly what it implies: something that has taken a strong hold of you. At this stage, it isn't so easy to weed it out. When wrong thoughts become strongholds in your life, they will choke your potential to flourish.

Resisting Temptation

'Blessed *is* the man who endures temptation;' (James 1:12)

The lure and trap of pornography, particularly on the Internet, is a perfect example of the progression we have been talking about. A 'seed thought' is entertained and allowed to develop into a 'stronghold' in the mind.

An individual falling into this trap begins by indulging a *thought*. Before long, they are *preoccupied* in their thought processes. Soon they are *arguing* that what they are involved in is acceptable and won't harm anyone. However, the tragedy of this behaviour is a 'not-easily-broken' *stronghold* that has been the demise of many individuals, marriages and families.

Temptation succeeds when someone is drawn away and enticed by their own desires, rather than God's purposes. What is 'more pleasant to their soul' overshadows what is right in the sight of God. James used the analogy of conception and birth, except that instead of life being established, death results – death to the purposes of God in your life. As James wrote:

> 'But each one is tempted when he is drawn away by his own desires
> and enticed. Then, when desire has conceived, it gives birth to sin;
> and sin, when it is full-grown, brings forth death.' (James 1:14-15)

Entertain an alluring thought for long enough and it won't stay a thought for long. If not dealt with immediately, it can become a fully-fledged lifestyle that is contrary to God's plans for a flourishing life.

Such deceptive illusions never show the whole picture or ramifications. The husband who is tempted to embark on an adulterous affair isn't focusing on the hurt and devastation, the financial loss, or feelings of shame and guilt that will come to his family.

Resisting temptation the moment you encounter it is essential, because it can quickly develop into a thriving issue or stronghold. Don't make the mistake of toying with it, because it *will* jeopardise your future.

A Flourishing Prayer Life

'Then He spoke a parable to them, that men always
ought to pray and not lose heart...' (Luke 18:1)

It is a presumptuous person who thinks they can live without prayer. Some people call themselves Christians but they never take the time to communicate with God. As a result, their relationship with Him fails to flourish in the way that it could or should.

God created us to know and enjoy the blessing of a personal relationship with Him. In the Garden of Eden, Adam walked and talked with God without inhibition, and it was only when sin separated him from God that he hid himself. Many people still hide from God today, not realising that through Jesus Christ they can be perfectly reconciled. This is what the Bible says: 'Then He spoke a parable to them, that men always ought to pray and not lose heart...' (Luke 18:1)

Sadly, there are many who find prayer difficult and the reason why they lose heart is because wrong perceptions or traditions about prayer keep them starved of a personal relationship with God.

Jesus was in constant communication with the Father and never acted without His instruction. We can also read how Jesus communicated with those who were close to Him. He didn't only teach His disciples spiritual truths, but He also talked naturally with them. They were able to be honest and open, and ask Him anything.

This is a wonderful pattern of what our relationship with God can be like. Your communication with Him need not be based on repetitious, religious prayers but instead you can enjoy a close, intimate relationship with Him. I enjoy taking time out to speak with the Lord while out running, driving my car or even sitting on an aeroplane. When your prayer life flourishes, you feel its effect across every area of your life.

Flourishing in the Midst of Opposition
'But he who endures to the end will be saved.' (Matthew 10:22)

When you begin to flourish in life, others will certainly notice – but not everyone will be happy about it. The blessing of God will draw the attention of others, but it will also attract its share of opposition. So what can you do in the midst of persecution?

• Commit to greater blessing
'For when tribulation or persecution arises because of the word, immediately he stumbles.' (Matthew 13:21) Our natural instinct would be to draw back, but be determined to stand your ground and refuse to lower your stand. In fact, why not commit to flourish even more in the face of persecution!

• Whistle a different tune
'But I say to you ... pray for those who spitefully use you and persecute you,' (Matthew 5:44) Instead of reacting according to the ways of the world, respond according to the way of the Word. Don't let those who persecute you rule your spirit but rather become an agent of blessing. It will keep your spirit free.

• Keep your course
'And you will be hated by all for My name's sake. But he who endures to the end will be saved.' (Matthew 10:22) No matter what you are facing, stay on course because God is faithful to His promises.

In the midst of persecution, refuse to draw back or allow others to rule your spirit. Having done all, stand and keep your course. The seeds of the highest quality that God has placed in you are destined to flourish and prosper. Don't settle for anything less. Let your life bear testimony to what you believe in and let others see those signs following.

How You Can Help Your Church Flourish

'But the children of Israel were fruitful and increased abundantly,
multiplied and grew exceedingly mighty...' (Exodus 1:7)

Human nature, when left to its own devices, is prone to settling down
and becoming comfortable. The biggest enemy to a flourishing life is
complacency, which is why every believer and every church needs a
commitment to maintain and empower the momentum.

The fact is that healthy things grow, so one of my highest priorities is to
keep our church healthy. It is complacency that makes Christianity and
church life dull and mediocre, but it is momentum that keeps people
moving forward to the next level. As Senior Pastor of a growing church,
here are five things that I believe you can do to help your church flourish.

• **Your testimony** - The Apostle Paul describes believers as 'living epistles'
who are 'known and read by all men.' When your life is flourishing in God,
others will be inspired by your testimony and example.

• **Your attention** - There is nothing more rewarding than preaching to a
receptive congregation. Don't allow yourself to go through the motions
at church, but always be hungry for the Word of God.

• **Your presence** - Would you be missed if you didn't make it to church?
The reality is that those who are growing in God not only attend church,
they presence themselves there and contribute to the atmosphere.

• **Your gifts and talents** - God uses the different strengths and talents
of individuals to add to the church. You have unique gifts that can build
your local church.

• **Your health** - Every church needs a core of people who are spiritually
healthy. Their words and example bring life and energy to the church.
Believe for God to bless you with a healthy spirit, mind and body so you
are unhindered in serving Him.

Determine Whether You Can Flourish

'For he shall be like a tree planted by the waters, which
spreads out its roots by the river...' (Jeremiah 17:8)

The decisions you make will position you to flourish or flounder in
life. Ask yourself the following questions and determine whether you are
positioned to thrive.

• Are you planted?

'For he shall be like a tree planted by the waters...' (Jeremiah 17:8)
If you are not planted anywhere, you will not grow. Likewise, if you are
planted in the wrong environment, you will not produce the best fruit.
A tree planted by the waters is in a good position to receive regular
nourishment.

Every believer needs to be planted in a local church where they can thrive
in their gifts and talents, and where there is plenty of encouragement and
room for growth. If you are planted in a place where you are limited and
contained, you are unlikely to see the seed of the highest quality within
you reach its full potential.

• How easily can you be uprooted?

'Which spreads out its roots by the river...' (Jeremiah 17:8)
When the roots of a tree are widely spread and run deep into the earth,
it is not easy to uproot or move them. It is the same with those who are
planted in God's House and are actively involved in the spectrum of church
life. They are the ones who are always there, participating in study groups,
helping with the children and youth, and financially committed to church
projects. Because their friendships and relationships are built around the
church family, it would be a great upheaval if they had to uproot themselves
and move away.

Compare these to those who stay on the fringe of church life and never
allow themselves to become completely involved or committed to
anything. It is easy for them to uproot themselves and drift away, preventing
themselves from flourishing the way God intended.

• **Can you take the heat?**
'And will not fear when heat comes....' (Jeremiah 17:8)
The Word doesn't say 'if heat comes' but 'when heat comes.' The Bible
never promises us a life without tests or challenges, and there will always
be obstacles to overcome. Let me assure you – the heat will come.

A flourishing life is not thrown off course by obstacles or a bit of heat. Don't
be like those who draw back when opposition comes their way – stand
firm. The psalmist wrote:

'We went through fire and through water;
But You brought us out to rich *fulfillment*.' (Psalm 66:12)

If you are planted in the House of the Lord, no matter what happens, you
can weather the storm. There will be times when you will go through the
fire, but you will emerge strong and victorious.

• **Is your spiritual health a priority?**
'But its leaf will be green,' (Jeremiah 17:8)
Lush, green foliage is the evidence of a healthy plant, but that doesn't
mean you stop watering it. You must commit to maintaining the health
of your spiritual life.

The reality is that the older we get, the harder it is to keep our level of
physical health and fitness. The same applies to our spiritual lives. Mature
Christians can think they know it all and that they don't have to apply
themselves as much as they used to in their spiritual growth.

Never take your spiritual life for granted, because you will lose your
strength and become weak. Don't neglect to feed your spirit daily. Today
there is so much resource available to build up your spirit and your local
church should be the place where you are constantly receiving spiritual
nourishment.

• **Are you ruled by the seasons?**

'And will not be anxious in the year of drought,' (Jeremiah 17:8)

Some people never move forward in life because they are ruled by the seasons. Many are ruled by the economic climate – whenever the dollar takes a dive, they become fearful about the future. Because their future hinges on these possibilities, they never invest any time or energy into building anything substantial.

Those who are planted in God's House are not afraid of dry seasons because they understand that seasons have an end. They are the ones who continue putting God first when their finances are tight or circumstances are rocky. Paul wrote: 'And let us not grow weary while doing good, for in due season we shall reap if we do not lose heart.' (Galatians 6:9)

• **Is fruitfulness a lifestyle?**

'Nor will cease from yielding fruit.' (Jeremiah 17:8)

Psalm 92 promises that those who are planted in the House of the Lord 'shall still bear fruit in old age.' There are those who only give to others when their circumstances are favourable, but for those who are planted in God's House, giving is a lifestyle. They give generously from the fruit of their lives, whether they are in or out of season.

The fact is that fruit that remains on a tree doesn't benefit anyone. Sadly, there are those who are fruitful but never surrender their fruit to bless others. Remember, God's will for His people to flourish and prosper goes further than our own lives.

You have every opportunity to flourish in the House of God if you choose to be planted and to allow your roots to go down deep. Be prepared to take the heat and to be consistent in the seasons. Always give your spiritual health priority, and build a lifestyle that is constantly blessing others with the fruit of your life.

Epilogue

When Bobbie and I moved to Australia in 1978, we had only been married a year. One could possibly see the seeds of potential within us, but we didn't have much fruit.

Nevertheless, we began sowing our lives into the work of the ministry because we had a vision and a dream to build a flourishing church. On Sunday August 14th 1983, we held our initial services in the Baulkham Hills School Hall with a congregation of only 45 people. At that time, we could never have imagined that decades later, we would be pastoring what is possibly Australia's largest church.

Over the years, we began to be fruitful and multiply, and thousands have come to know Christ through our weekend services. When I look across our congregation each week, it blesses me to see the many people who decided to plant themselves in God's House and have gone from strength to strength. The result is that they are 'fresh and flourishing' and the fruit of their lives is evident to all.

Who could have foreseen the number of lives that have been impacted by Hillsong Church? Such an abundance of fruit and increase is only known to God.

The fact is that *you can count how many seeds there are in an orange, but you cannot count how many oranges there are in a seed.*

God has deposited seeds of the highest quality within you that have the potential to build a flourishing life beyond your greatest dreams. My prayer is that you will plant yourself in a local church where you will be nourished and bring forth all that is within you.

Brian Houston

BOOK FOUR

HOW TO MAKE WISE CHOICES

PRINCIPLES FOR BUILDING
A LIFE OF WISDOM

HOW TO MAXIMISE YOUR LIFE

The Question of Wisdom
'Ask! What shall I give you?' (2 Chronicles 1:7)

If God presented you with this question, 'Ask! What shall I give you?' what would you reply?

The Bible tells how one night God appeared to Solomon, the Hebrew king who lived some 3,000 years ago, and asked him this very question. Solomon could have requested fame, fortune, longevity or world domination, but this is what he said:

> 'Now give me wisdom and knowledge, that I may go out and come in before this people; for who can judge this great people of Yours?' (2 Chronicles 1:10)

That simple request for wisdom was the key to everything else Solomon could ever want in life. In ruling wisely, he achieved great fame, fortune and success – for both himself and the kingdom.

If wisdom is the key to everything you could ever want in life, then what is it and how do you get it? The good news is that you don't have to be a silver-haired old sage or meditate under a tree of enlightenment to achieve wisdom. Under-rated by many but so vital for a blessed and successful life, wisdom is available to anyone who desires it.

There are those who think the Bible is full of rules, but it is a book of wisdom that embraces the entire spectrum of life. In essence, it teaches us how to live life well. Simply put, wisdom can be described as God's Word applied.

King Solomon's wisdom is still legendary today and throughout the book of Proverbs, he contrasts the life choices of a wise person with those of a foolish person. Making the right decisions in life is the result of wisdom, and choosing wisdom, as Solomon did, is the starting point.

Keys to Finding Wisdom

\Wis"dom\ (-d[u^]m), n.
1. The quality of being wise; knowledge, and the capacity to make due use of it; knowledge of the best ends and the best means; discernment and judgement; discretion; sagacity; skill; dexterity. (Websters Revised Unabridged Dictionary)

Choosing Wisdom

'Wisdom *is* the principle thing; *therefore* get wisdom.' (Proverbs 4:7)

Undoubtedly Solomon's wisest choice was to request wisdom. He could have asked God for anything but the fact is that Solomon valued wisdom and considered it his greatest asset in life. Here is a profound piece of advice from this wise king: 'Wisdom *is* the principle thing; *therefore* get wisdom.' (Proverbs 4:7)

Solomon considered wisdom to be the most important thing you can obtain in life – so how do you 'get wisdom'? You cannot study for a degree in wisdom because it surpasses knowledge or intellect. For instance, a learned professor with a string of academic achievements may have unsurpassed knowledge in his field, but he may not be living wisely. He could have a history of broken relationships or financial disasters.

Wisdom can be defined as sound judgement or discretion. It includes what is colloquially referred to as 'common sense' (but the trouble with common sense is that it isn't all that common). God created us in His image and provided us with everything we need to succeed in life. Yet He also gave us the freedom of choice.

> 'I call heaven and earth as witnesses today against you, *that* I have set before you life and death, blessing and cursing; therefore choose life, that both you and your descendants may live;' (Deuteronomy 30:19)

If you stand facing the path to life and the path to death, which one would you choose? This should not be a difficult question – common sense would choose life, yet it is amazing how many people vacillate in their decision. Therefore, God, in His infinite wisdom, makes it abundantly clear which one to choose. Simply, wisdom begins with a choice. By making His wisdom available to us, God has set us up to succeed, yet it is in choosing wisdom that we take the initial step on the path to a successful life.

Two Gates, Two Destinations

'Enter by the narrow gate; for wide *is* the gate and broad *is*
the way that leads to destruction...' (Matthew 7:13)

Have you ever stood at a fork in the road and wondered which path you should take? How do you make your decision? Jesus Christ said this: 'Enter by the narrow gate; for wide *is* the gate and broad *is* the way that leads to destruction, and there are many who go in by it.' (Matthew 7:13)

Jesus was speaking about two gates that lead to two destinations – the narrow gate that leads to life and the wide gate that leads to death. The scriptures often speak of these two contrasting paths and their subsequent destinations. When the Bible talks about death, it is often referring to the death of our future and potential. There is a proverb that says:

'There is a way *that seems* right to a man, but its end *is* the way of death.' (Proverbs 14:12)

Many choose to enter by the wide gate because it 'seems right' but in the end their dreams and potential are never realised. A gate is a point of entry that leads to a specific destination, and this is where wisdom is so pivotal to your future. Instead of taking the way that seems right, we need to know the way that is right. Solomon wrote of wisdom:

'She takes her stand on top of the high hill,
Beside the way, where the paths meet.
She cries out by the gates, at the entry of the city,
At the entrance of the doors:' (Proverbs 8:2-3)

As you encounter the many crossroads in life, be assured that wisdom is crying out to be applied. It cries out to you when you need it the most – before you embark on the journey. One wise choice can be the turning point that will set you on the right path that will lead upwards towards the kind of life God intended. As the Bible declares, 'The way of life *winds* upward for the wise' (Proverbs 15:24).

The Brighter Path

'But the path of the just *is* like the shining sun.' (Proverbs 4:18)

It has been said that there are three ways to learn: the easy way, the hard way, and the tragic way. The easy way is to learn from other people's mistakes, the hard way is to learn from your own mistakes, but the tragic way is not to learn from either. The difference between a wise and unwise person is that, simply put, a foolish person never learns from his mistakes. Solomon's description of the contrasting paths illustrates the pattern of their lives:

> 'But the path of the just *is* like the shining sun,
> That shines ever brighter unto the perfect day.
> The way of the wicked *is* like darkness;
> They do not know what makes them stumble.' (Proverbs 4:18-19)

The brighter path of the righteous is in direct contrast to the deep gloom that clouds the other path. Those on the darkened path cannot see clearly and stumble over every obstacle that life may present. When the Bible talks about the 'wicked', it isn't necessarily referring to people who are evil, but to those whose decisions have set them on the wrong path. Over time, the direction they are heading in may eventually cause them to become entrenched in the destructive ways of the Wicked One (Satan).

You may know people who go from strength to strength, in contrast to others who lurch from one crisis to another. Perhaps their experience has been one failed relationship after another, or one financial disaster followed by yet another. They never seem to break the cycle and keep making the same mistakes over and over again. They cannot see what keeps tripping them up or making them stumble.

Learning from a mistake is a positive thing, but if someone believes that they are a victim of circumstances, they won't realise that by changing the way they are going they can turn their life around. God's wisdom will lead you down the path of life. His intention for your life and future is that it gets brighter and brighter, like the shining sun.

Taking the Wrong Path

'Blessed *is* the man who walks not in the
counsel of the ungodly...' (Psalm 1:1)

You never arrive at a particular destination by accident. Life is a series of decisions that carry us in a certain direction. The psalmist describes such a progression, 'Blessed *is* the man who walks not in the counsel of the ungodly, nor stands in the path of sinners, nor sits in the seat of the scornful' (Psalm 1:1). Someone may begin to walk down a destructive path when they accept unwise advice. Wisdom may be crying out but they do not hear it. If their ear is tuned elsewhere and they listen to ungodly counsel long enough, they may find themself adopting the same stance and sitting in the same cynical seat. A progressive journey down the wrong path can find someone saying, 'I'd never thought I'd find myself here!'

Even believers can fall into this trap if areas of their lives are not in line with the wisdom of God. Perhaps they have a wonderful marriage and family, but they lack wisdom in their financial affairs. They can sabotage their family's future because they keep tripping up on that one issue. We need to apply wisdom to every area of our lives. Your thinking is critical in determining which path you are on and can easily start you on a path that progressively spirals downward.

> 'For the weapons of our warfare *are* not carnal but mighty in God for pulling down strongholds, casting down arguments and every high thing that exalts itself against the knowledge of God, bringing every thought into captivity to the obedience of Christ,' (2 Corinthians 10:4-5).

The verse describes a powerful progression. Entertain a particular thought long enough and it will become a 'high thing' that preoccupies and dominates your mind. Leave it unchecked and it then becomes an argument. Quite literally, it makes such sense to you that you would argue to defend it. Ultimately it becomes a stronghold, which means exactly that – it has a strong hold over your life. Maybe you find yourself on the wrong path, but be encouraged. By applying God's wisdom to your situation, you can begin to walk the path God has set before you.

Wisdom at the Crossroads

'She takes her stand on top of the high hill, beside
the way, where the paths meet.' (Proverbs 8:2)

How often have you heard people say, 'If only I had made a different decision?' It is amazing how everything seems so much clearer in hindsight. The reality is that you don't often see the consequences of your choices until further down the track. While it may not be possible to change your past, you can change your future. Wisdom is always crying out to bring positive change in our lives.

'Does not wisdom cry out, and understanding lift up her voice? She takes her stand on top of the high hill, beside the way, where the paths meet.' (Proverbs 8:1-2)

The place where two paths meet is significant because this is when the road on which you are travelling comes to an intersection or a crossroad. It is here that you have the opportunity to make a powerful choice – to stay on the same path or change direction.

I have heard many people testify about the time they came to a crossroad in life and changed the course of their future. Those who were heading down a road to destruction and ruin heard wisdom crying out and changed direction. They are blessed and flourishing today because of one significant and courageous choice.

Not only does wisdom cry out to you at the crossroads but she also takes a stand 'on the top of the high hill.' You may think that greater wisdom is required when you are struggling at the bottom of a hill, but the fact is that the higher you go and the taller you stand, the more wisdom you need. The larger and more influential your life becomes, the greater the ramifications of every decision.

Wisdom is available to you whenever you need it. All you have to do is ask: 'If any of you lacks wisdom, let him ask of God, who gives to all liberally and without reproach, and it will be given to him.' (James 1:5)

Wisdom for the Street

'Wisdom calls aloud outside; she raises her
voice in the open squares.' (Proverbs 1:20)

Solomon's desire for wisdom went beyond himself and his own gain. He
wanted wisdom to rule with integrity over the people God had called him
to lead. Wisdom is essential to be effective and influential in the world we
live in. Some 'religious' people fear the outside world and try to protect
themselves by separating themselves from any kind of external influence.
They completely miss the point that, as believers, we are called to live a
life of influence that goes beyond our own existence. The wisdom of God
is not only applicable for our private inner life but can be applied in the
everyday circumstances we face. Solomon wrote:

> 'Wisdom calls aloud outside; she raises her voice in the open
> squares. She cries out in the chief concourses, at the openings of
> the gates in the city' (Proverbs 1:20-21).

• **Outside** – Wisdom enables us to be street-wise or street-savvy, rather
than gullible and naive.

• **Open squares** – This refers to places of business and trade, where
negotiations and deals are being made. Wisdom is raising her voice
regarding your career, your work situation and has the power to equip
you for the marketplace.

• **Chief concourses** – You can know wisdom along the major
thoroughfares of your life. Wisdom helps keep you on the right path and
prevents you from diverting and ending up down some dead-end side alley.
When it comes to your career, business or ministry encounters, wisdom
is there to guide you.

• **Gates** – In ancient times, the only entrance to a walled city was through
the gates. It was the point of entry for all kinds of resource and supply.
Through wisdom we can choose what we permit to enter our lives.

Wisdom is available inside and outside – equipping us in both our personal,
internal world and our day-to-day external world.

WISDOM BUILDS THE HOUSE

'Through wisdom a house is built,
And by understanding it is established;
By knowledge the rooms are filled
With all precious and pleasant riches.'
(Proverbs 24:3-4)

Wisdom Builds the House

'Through wisdom a house is built, and by
understanding it is established' (Proverbs 24:3)

The construction of a building isn't based on guesswork or luck. Building a dream house depends on carefully following detailed architectural plans. In the same way, your life can be compared to building a house.

The foundation on which you build determines what is established. When people attempt to build their lives on a **poor foundation, dysfunction,** disappointment and 'rooms' filled with sadness and strife are the result. On the other hand, building on wisdom establishes a strong foundation.

We are all in the process of building our lives, so what plans are you following? The psalmist wrote, 'Unless the LORD builds the house, they labor in vain who build it' (Psalm 127:1).

How sad to get to the end of your life and discover you could have built your life a better way. It reminds me of the story Jesus told about two men who each built themself a house. The house of the wise man was built on the rock. Storms, floods and gale-force winds shook the house, but it remained standing because its foundations were strong. Compare this to the other house:

> 'But everyone who hears these sayings of Mine, and does not do them, will be like a foolish man who built his house on the sand: and the rain descended, the floods came, and the winds blew and beat on that house; and it fell. And great was its fall.' (Matthew 7:26-27)

You may know people who face one challenge after another but remain strong while others fall apart. When you apply the wisdom of God and allow Him to build your house (your life), you will withstand the storms of life and come out on top every time.

Building on Wrong Foundations

'All things are lawful for me, but all things
are not helpful.' (1 Corinthians 6:12)

The man who built his house on the sand made the mistake of underestimating the importance of foundations. Many fall into the trap of building on something that *seems* right instead of what *is* right.

There are those who attempt to build their lives on rules and regulations, assuming that if they keep all the rules, they cannot go wrong. Laws are necessary, but they can keep people so focused on what they cannot do that they never look at what they can do. The Bible says: 'All things are lawful for me, but all things are not helpful.' (1 Corinthians 6:12)

Rules will always look at what is lawful but wisdom will focus on what is helpful or beneficial. Some will see the Bible as a book of confining rules instead of a book of wisdom and principles for living life well. Instead of living by rigidly enforced rules and regulations, wisdom causes us to set good boundaries for our own lives. For example, Solomon wrote:

'My son, eat honey because *it is* good,
And the honeycomb *which is* sweet to your taste;' (Proverbs 24:13)

In this proverb, he states the virtues of eating honey because it is good and sweet, but in the following chapter, Solomon states:

'Have you found honey?
Eat only as much as you need,
Lest you be filled with it and vomit.' (Proverbs 25:16)

From these verses, it appears that health and harm can come from the same honey-jar. Therefore discretion is needed. Many things in excess can be damaging, and 'honey' may represent one of these in your own life. Some would legislate that the 'honey' should be banned altogether, while others will exercise no self-discipline whatsoever. Rather than being extreme one way or the other, wisdom teaches us restraint and the value of building healthy, liberating parameters in our lives.

Wisdom About Wealth

'He who trusts in his riches will fall, but the righteous
will flourish like foliage.' (Proverbs 11:28)

Statistics show that more marriages and relationships break down over finance than any other issue. Sadly, many make the mistake of building their lives around money and the pursuit of wealth. The reality is you cannot expect to build your house on riches because it will not stand. Godly wisdom warns us against trusting in money because it is an unstable foundation. Solomon wrote:

'He who trusts in his riches will fall, but the righteous will flourish like foliage.' (Proverbs 11:28)

When Solomon chose wisdom above anything else, God said: '...I will give you riches and wealth and honor, such as none of the kings have had who *were* before you, nor shall any after you have the like.' (2 Chronicles 1:12)

Amazingly, Solomon's wealth is as legendary as his wisdom, but his trust wasn't in his riches. Contrary to some thinking, God is not against us having money – He is against money having us. You can have wisdom AND wealth, but the key is our *attitude* to wealth and finance. The Bible wisely cautions us:

- Do not *trust* in uncertain riches (1 Timothy 6:17);
- Do not *love* money – it is 'the root of all *kinds of* evil' (1 Timothy 6:10);
- Do not *desire* to be rich or lust after money – those who desire to be rich 'fall into temptation and a snare' (1 Timothy 6:9);
- Do not *serve* money – 'You cannot serve God and mammon (money)' (Matthew 6:24); and
- Do not *pursue* money – '...the rich man also will fade away in his pursuits.' (James 1:11)

Money makes a great servant but is a terrible master. Money won't build your life, but with wisdom, you will see finance an effective tool and resource.

Progression to Wisdom

'Discretion will preserve you; understanding
will keep you.' (Proverbs 2:11)

The question begs to be asked, why would anyone ignore wisdom when it is crying out to be heard? Yet people do all the time. If someone has ventured down the wrong path, wisdom can be shouting at them, but they do not hear it because their ear isn't tuned to it. So how does wisdom change your course? Solomon outlines this in the following verse:

'When wisdom enters your heart, and knowledge is pleasant to your soul, discretion will preserve you; understanding will keep you, to deliver you from the way of evil...' (Proverbs 2:10-12)

• **Knowledge that is 'pleasant to your soul.'** By law, cigarette packets are required to clearly contain the warning 'Harmful to your health.' You may know that to be true but do you have the wisdom to apply what you know? Knowledge will be tested by what is more 'pleasant' or agreeable to your emotions, thinking and will. Knowing is the first step.

• **Understanding that 'will keep you.'** Wisdom does not come by knowing or understanding alone. You can know and understand a principle but unless you apply it, nothing will change. Someone with a drinking or gambling problem may know and understand that their habit is destroying their family and future, but if their addiction is more agreeable to their soul, they will continue down that destructive path.

• **Discretion that 'will preserve you.'** Discretion is both good taste and good sense. When someone makes the decision to apply knowledge and understanding, then discretion kicks in and keeps them from harm.

• **Wisdom 'enters your heart.'** Ultimately wisdom enters your life when you find knowledge and understanding agreeable to your heart, and you have the good sense to apply it to your life.

Wise Words

'The lips of the righteous feed many, but fools
die for lack of wisdom.' (Proverbs 10:21)

What is inside will come out. If wisdom has entered your heart, wisdom should come out of your mouth. Jesus put it this way, 'For out of the abundance of the heart the mouth speaks.' (Matthew 12:34)

Many of the proverbs written by Solomon describe the contrast between the words of the wise and the speech of fools. He wrote, 'Wisdom is found on the lips of him who has understanding, but a rod *is* for the back of him who is devoid of understanding.' (Proverbs 10:13)

You may recall words of great wisdom that impacted your life, yet there may also be words that were more like a rod on your back. Perhaps the critical words of a parent or a teacher may still ring in your ears? Sadly, there are even some preachers who batter their congregation with guilt and condemnation, instead of bringing words of life.

Words are so powerful that the Bible declares that life and death are in the power of the tongue. We need to carefully select which words we receive and take to heart, yet we also need to be aware of the power of the words we speak. Solomon said, 'The lips of the righteous feed many, but fools die for lack of wisdom.' (Proverbs 10:21)

If the people around you depend on your words for nourishment, I hope they are not dying of malnutrition. Children who have been raised without any encouragement grow up lacking confidence and starving for attention. The lack of nourishing words can bring death to their potential. Just as those who are starving will scratch for food in garbage bins, those who are emotionally malnourished will seek comfort wherever they can find it. Sadly, it is often in all the wrong places.

Marriages and relationships begin to starve to death when partners continually run each other down, instead of lifting each other up. Wisdom recognises the need to constantly feed those around us with life-giving words.

135

Receiving Words of Wisdom

'My son, if you receive my words...' (Proverbs 2:1)

When I embarked on my chosen career path, I noticed people were quick to pigeonhole or box me. Their words could have limited me from going beyond their expectations. I know that God's will for every one of us is an enlarged, expansive life so I chose not to accept their words or limiting perception of life.

It is not only the words we speak but the words we *receive* that affect our future. We are surrounded by an endless barrage of words, opinions and information so we need to be wise about what we take on board. Do you know that you give power to whatever you receive or accept in life – whether positive or negative? The Bible says , 'But to as many as did receive *and* welcome Him, He gave the authority (power, privilege, right) to become the children of God...' (John 1:12 AMP)

The context of the original Greek describes receiving Jesus in terms of gaining power or authority. **What you receive, you empower.** If you accept words that limit or contain you, you empower them. They become the authority that dictates the boundaries or parameters of your life. For instance, a child who is told that they are useless, will more than likely grow up with a low self-esteem. Wisdom teaches us that there are words that we should receive and words that are unacceptable. Solomon wrote: 'The wise in heart will receive commands, but a prating fool will fall.' (Proverbs 10:8)

When you receive negative words, they are empowered to dictate the course of your life. Many people accepted negative words spoken over them and years later are still contained by them. To break their power, they need to reject what was spoken and replace them with new, godly words that build a bigger, more expansive life. The Bible says, 'Listen to counsel and receive instruction, that you may be wise in your latter days.' (Proverbs 19:20)

Hence, positioning yourself to receive positive, life-giving words is an essential key to building a life of wisdom.

Wise Inclinations

'So that you incline your ear to wisdom...' (Proverbs 2:2)

Have you ever leaned on a seemingly stable object and it toppled over, causing you to stumble or fall? The fact is, the way you lean determines the way you fall.

You probably know people who always seem to land on their feet regardless of circumstances, whereas others fall flat on their faces. Everyone is entitled to their partialities and preferences, but your 'leanings' or inclinations can build or break your life.

Are you more inclined towards a positive or negative viewpoint? Solomon wrote about 'inclining your ear' to wisdom.

'Incline your ear and hear the words of the wise...' (Proverbs 22:17)

What you incline your ear towards affects not only the way you hear but the way you live. Some people are more prone to negativity because that is what they incline their ear towards, eagerly listening to gossip or criticism. Some people eagerly declare, 'Everybody's saying...' when the reality is that 'everybody' may only be two or three people. Where they are positioned determines what they hear and because their inclination is towards those two or three, it really seems like everybody.

What you hear is what you receive. Jesus stated , 'Take heed what you hear. With the same measure you use, it will be measured to you...' (Mark 4:24).

We all rate what we hear by our own measurement scale. On a scale of 1-10, you may rate what you hear on the news as an 8 and what you hear in church as a 3. Because your inclination is higher towards the television, you will remember and receive that more than the wisdom you hear in church.

Yet if it is God's wisdom you incline yourself towards and position yourself to hear, that is what you will receive. And if that's the way you lean, guess which way you are going to land?

Discernment
'Yes, if you cry out for discernment...' (Proverbs 2:3)

The Bible tells how Solomon needed to make a difficult judgement between the conflicting stories of two women who were arguing over the possession of a baby. Eventually he resolved what to do.

He called for a sword and commanded the infant to be cut in half. Instantly the real mother was identified as her protective maternal instinct surfaced – she was prepared to give up the child to the other woman rather than see him harmed in any way. Solomon knew that to judge people wisely, he needed the ability to correctly discern the truth. When he asked God for wisdom, he specifically said: 'Therefore give to Your servant an understanding heart to judge Your people, that I may discern between good and evil.' (1 Kings 3:9)

To discern is the ablity to read or perceive a situation correctly. Life is filled with situations that cry out for discernment and many mistakes are made because people make bad judgements. Jesus cautioned us about making surface assessments or judgements: 'Do not judge according to appearance, but judge with righteous judgement.' (John 7:24)

Jesus instructs us to judge with 'righteous judgement' – a quality which is in essence, discernment. It is not our place to judge people's motives or heart (because that is God's job) but what we can do is assess their track record or actions.

Judging by appearance is not only dangerous but foolish. So often people are captivated by surface issues such as another's good looks or talent, but fail to look at their chequered history.

Discernment is less about judging and more about reading situations correctly. Instead of judging by appearances, wisdom will enable you to look below the surface and discern the truth.

Speaking Up

'...lift up your voice for understanding...' (Proverbs 2:3)

We have all experienced occasions when we opened our mouths and said something inappropriate. Unfortunately, once the words are out, there isn't a lot you can do to get them back. According to the Bible, taming the tongue is one of the greatest challenges of all.

'If anyone does not stumble in word, he *is* a perfect man, able also to bridle the whole body.' (James 3:2)

Our lives are not only impacted by what we hear, but also by what we say (or don't say, for that matter). Solomon wrote that there is 'a time to keep silence, and a time to speak' (Ecclesiastes 3:7). Often we confuse those times, which is why we need wisdom to know when we should or shouldn't lift up our voices. For instance, there is a proverb that says this:

'He who blesses his friend with a loud voice, rising early in the morning, It will be counted a curse to him.' (Proverbs 27:14)

Clearly, raising your voice at the wrong time can have disastrous consequences. People will often lift their voice to express their opinions but there are times when it is not wise to give your opinion. Certainly, everyone has a right to their opinion but opinions don't build lives. Wisdom builds the house!

So when should we raise our voice? Solomon instructed us, 'lift up your voice for understanding' (Proverbs 2:3). The time to speak up boldly is when we see injustice or when a friend's character is being assassinated. As Christians, we need to speak up for the sake of the Gospel. The Apostle Paul was jailed and beaten because he refused to stop preaching the Gospel.

Finally, wisdom tells us to raise our voices when we cry out to God in need and when we praise Him. 'I cry out to the LORD with my voice; with my voice to the LORD I make my supplication.' (Psalm 142:1)

Wisdom Versus Age and Experience
'Remember now your Creator in the days of your youth,
Before the difficult days come...' (Ecclesiastes 12:1)

At the age of seventeen, I encountered a man in his late forties on the streets of Wanganui, New Zealand, who said to me, 'You wait until you are my age and you'll see things differently.' Being young and full of hope for the future, I was amazed someone could be so full of negativity and cynicism. He had obviously experienced some bitter twists and turns on his path through life and reckoned he had 'seen it all'.

There are many like him who are so experienced in hurt and pain that they don't believe things can be any different. They allow their past experiences to limit their future. The Bible cautions us, 'Remember now your Creator in the days of your youth, before the difficult days come, and the years draw near when you say, "I have no pleasure in them."' (Ecclesiastes 12:1)

The older someone gets and the more 'difficult days' they experience, the more cynical they can become. Who is more experienced about marriage – someone who has been married and divorced five times, or someone who has been married once and still going strong after twenty-five years?

Experience is not always a positive. If your experience is contrary to the Word of God, it can be a severe limitation, so never bring the level of your belief down to the level of your experience.

The reality is that experience won't build your life – but wisdom will. Don't allow your outlook on life to be clouded or limited by your experience; nor allow age to prevent you from building a great life. The Bible tells how Jesus Christ was twelve years old when He sat in the Temple in Jerusalem, surrounded by the religious leaders and teachers of the day. It says , 'And all who heard Him were astonished at His understanding and answers.' (Luke 2:47)

His wisdom couldn't be credited to age or experience yet Jesus amazed them with His understanding. No matter what your age or experience, choose to build your life according to the principles of God.

Applying Understanding

'...apply your heart to understanding...' (Proverbs 2:2)

A friend who was taking part in our annual fund-raising Fun Run once told me how he had been the high school track champion. Although he hadn't trained for over five years, he believed he would easily complete the 5km distance. He may have once had the athletic ability to run that distance with ease but because he hadn't applied himself in recent years, he struggled.

It is one thing to have knowledge but unless you *apply* it, it won't do you any good. Raw talent can only take you so far in life, and to be successful, you have to apply yourself. To 'apply' means to 'put into action'. The best description of wisdom that I know is 'God's Word applied' (i.e. putting God's Word into action). The Bible instructs us, 'apply your heart to understanding' (Proverbs 2:2).

Many people prefer ignorance because understanding involves responsibility. For instance, on our first trip to the USA, we were pulled over by a policeman. He looked at my driver's licence and asked, 'Don't they have road rules in Australia?' Knowing that understanding involves responsiblity, my immediate thought was to act ignorant, and say 'Excusi? Non comprehendo!' (But I didn't, and took responsibility for my actions!)

Understanding takes away any excuses and makes you accountable. There are some Christians who know what the Bible says but nothing changes in their lives because they don't want to deal with certain issues. The moment you understand that God has given you the answers, you are responsible for applying His counsel in your life.

A wise person will assume the responsibility for their own life and apply themself to grow in understanding. As a modern translation of the Bible aptly says:

> 'You know your way around the faith. Now do what you've been taught. School's out; quit studying the subject and start living it! And let your living spill over into thanksgiving.' (Colossians 2:7 The Message)

Always Willing to Learn

'A wise *man* will hear and increase learning...' (Proverbs 1:5)

One of the great keys to building a strong life is having a constant hunger and desire to learn more. It is a foolish person who thinks he knows it all. As William Shakespeare put it, 'The fool doth think he is wise, but the wise man knows himself to be a fool.' (As You Like It, Act 5 Scene 1)

Similarly, there is also a proverb that says, 'A wise *man* will hear and increase learning' (Proverbs 1:5). A wise person is one who never stops learning and is always eager to discover new things. Technology today enables us to access information faster than ever before, yet some members of the older generation are resistant to embrace unfamiliar methods. For example, they frown at the use of electric guitars or multi-media as a contemporary means of communication in church.

An ever-teachable spirit is characteristic of a wise person. The Bible tells how Joseph and Mary went looking for twelve-year-old Jesus: '...they found Him in the temple, sitting in the midst of the teachers, both listening to them and asking them questions.' (Luke 2:46)

We should never stop asking questions in life – there is always so much more to learn. As a German proverb says, 'To question a wise man is the beginning of wisdom.'

The disciples of Jesus spent over three years learning from His teachings and His example. Who would have thought that a humble fisherman or a despised tax collector could be transformed into a powerful Apostle of Jesus Christ? They opened their hearts to learn from the Master.

Learning is a major building block that will keep expanding your life. As this proverb states:

> 'Give *instruction* to a wise *man*, and he will be still wiser;
> Teach a just *man*, and he will increase in learning.' (Proverbs 9:9)

A WEALTH
OF WISDOM

'Happy *is* the man *who* finds wisdom,
And the man *who* gains understanding;
For her proceeds *are* better
than the profits of silver,
And her gain than fine gold.
She *is* more precious than rubies,
And all the things you may desire
cannot compare with her.'
(Proverbs 3:13-15)

Treasure Hunting

'If you seek her as silver, and search for
her as *for* hidden treasures;' (Proverbs 2:4)

There is something exciting about a treasure-hunt. All energy and focus is geared towards finding the prize at the end. It is interesting that Solomon compared wisdom to a treasure hunt by saying:

'...seek for her as silver, and search for her as *for* hidden treasures;'
(Proverbs 2:4)

Many people give their lives to the pursuit of their treasure, seeking after love, money or fame in a quest for happiness or fulfilment. Yet without wisdom, love, wealth or fame can result in emptiness or devastation. For example, the Betty Ford Clinic would contain the names of many famous drug addicts and rich, yet very lonely people with a history of failed relationships. All their money and fame didn't provide the fulfilment or security they obviously thought it would.

Contrary to some beliefs, God is not against fame or wealth. He gave Solomon 'riches and honour' such as none had had before him, and none after him. Since Solomon's greatest treasure was wisdom, he had the ability to see these other things for what they were – additional resource with which he could make a difference.

The pursuit of money or fame won't build your life, but they are counted among the rewards of God's wisdom because they have purpose. In His promise of blessing to Abraham, God said, 'I will bless you and make your name great; and you shall be a blessing.' (Genesis 12:2)

The purpose of Abraham's influence and wealth was that he was in a position to 'be a blessing' – to bless others. Godly wisdom causes you to see and live well beyond yourself. If you want lasting treasure in your life, let wisdom be your pursuit. As Solomon described her value:

'For her proceeds *are* better than the profits of silver, and her gain than fine gold. She *is* more precious than rubies, and all the things you may desire cannot compare with her.' (Proverbs 3:14-15)

Treasure Within

'...treasure my commands within you...' (Proverbs 2:1)

Some 400 years before Christ, the Ancient Greek playwright, Sophocles wrote, 'Wisdom outweighs any wealth.' Much has been said about wisdom and wealth, but the two often go hand in hand. The Bible says: 'So King Solomon surpassed all the kings of the earth in riches and wisdom.' (2 Chronicles 9:22)

Solomon's wealth was instrumental in building the kingdom in his day. His material riches have since passed away, yet it is the wealth of his wisdom that still impacts people today. The Bible, which contains Solomon's Proverbs, remains the best-selling book of all time. This is the indestructible treasure Jesus spoke about:

'Do not lay up for yourselves treasures on earth, where moth and rust destroy and thieves break in and steal; but lay up for yourselves treasures in heaven... For where your treasure is, there your heart will be also.' (Matthew 6:19-21)

Ultimately, wisdom is really an issue of the heart. Your heart will always leap toward your treasure, so if your heart is set on God's wisdom, you will prize it most highly.

Obtaining the priceless commodity called wisdom requires an understanding of where to look for it. Solomon gave us a clue: '...treasure my commands within you ...' (Proverbs 2:1)

The Bible often speaks of the 'treasure within.' Jesus said: 'A good man out of the good treasure of his heart brings forth good; and an evil man out of the evil treasure of his heart brings forth evil.' (Luke 6:45)

If good treasure (i.e. wisdom) is inside you, that is what will be reflected in your life. When you value wisdom as the greatest treasure of all, your heart will automatically be drawn to God and His Word.

Increase and Expansion

'And the Child grew and became strong in spirit,
filled with wisdom...' (Luke 2:40)

Take a young man who has aspirations of becoming a great leader in his field. Perhaps his dream is to head up a large corporation or even lead a nation. Starting out, he may not have much experience but it is applied wisdom that will build his reputation and credibility, causing others to follow his lead.

I believe Jesus Christ is the ultimate example of great leadership. From leading a small group of twelve disciples, today He has billions of faithful followers. Yet look back at the life of young Jesus. The Bible says, 'And the Child grew and became strong in spirit, filled with wisdom...' (Luke 2:40)

At the age of twelve, Jesus was 'filled with wisdom' but interestingly, some verses later, it says this, 'And Jesus increased in wisdom and stature'. (Luke 2:52)

One might think that if you are filled with wisdom, there is no room for more expansion. It is obviously possible that you can be full of wisdom yet still increase your capacity for more. Many people stop growing when they think they are full, and sadly, that is when they begin to decline.

Wisdom will always bring increase and expansion to your life. There will be an increase in blessing but there will also be an increase in challenges. The taller you stand and the higher you go, the more opposition you will face. The reality is that as your life enlarges, you will need a lot more wisdom because there is so much more at stake.

No matter how full of wisdom you may think you are, there is always room for more. The supply or store of wisdom will never run out, as the Bible says: 'He stores up sound wisdom for the upright;' (Proverbs 2:7)

'Sound wisdom' is dependable and will never let us down. We need to live our lives in a way that continually cries out for more wisdom. All we have to do is 'ask of God who gives to all liberally.'

Status and Favour

'And Jesus increased in wisdom and stature,
and in favor with God and men.' (Luke 2:52)

We all have people who inspire us to greater things by the example of their lives. A life built on wisdom is always a great example or model to follow. When others see the fruit or rewards of wisdom in your life, they will want what you've got. People saw things in Jesus, who was (and is) the personification of wisdom. The Bible says of Him: 'And Jesus increased in wisdom and stature, and in favor with God and men.' (Luke 2:52)

One of the rewards of wisdom will be increased stature and favour. Stature refers to one's size or status. By living according to God's wisdom, you will (not may) enlarge and grow. And when you keep God's commandments, you can expect this:

'*And* so find favor and high esteem
In the sight of God and man.' (Proverbs 3:4)

Such 'favour and high esteem' is not a result of pursuing the admiration or approval of people, it is a proceed of wisdom. Some try so hard to be accepted or liked by everybody – but that isn't possible, particularly if you want to become all God has destined you to be. You cannot live your life tiptoeing around others in case you offend them. True favour is when the people who you need to like and support you, do.

The ultimate benefit of wisdom is the favour of God. There are those who try to win His favour through their deeds, but His favour (His grace) is not a tap which is turned on or off, depending on what we do. His grace and favour is constant – the tap is always turned on. Now there may be kinks in the hose but wisdom tells us what we need to do to iron them out so there is a free flow. Having the favour of God doesn't mean there will be an absence of challenges or opposition, but you will have the grace and capacity to come through.

Proceeds of Wisdom

'Length of days *is* in her right hand, in her left
hand riches and honor.' (Proverbs 3:16)

The Bible records many promises of God (or 'proceeds') that wisdom will add to your life. Here is a list of twelve contained in Proverbs 3 and 4:

1. Happiness
'Happy *is* the man *who* finds wisdom' (Proverbs 3:13)

2. Long life and longevity
'Length of days *is* in her right hand' (Proverbs 3:16)

3. Riches and honour
'In her left hand riches and honor' (Proverbs 3:16)

4. Pleasantness and peace
'Her ways *are* ways of pleasantness, and all her paths *are* peace'
(Proverbs 3:17)

5. Safety and security
'Then you will walk safely in your way' (Proverbs 3:23)

6. A stumble-free walk
'And your foot will not stumble' (Proverbs 3:23)

7. Free of anxiety
'When you lie down, you will not be afraid' (Proverbs 3:24)

8. Sweet sleep
'Yes, you will lie down and your sleep will be sweet' (Proverbs 3:24)

9. Protection in a sudden crisis or calamity
'Do not be afraid of sudden terror' (Proverbs 3:25)

10. Confidence
'For the LORD will be your confidence' (Proverbs 3:26)

11. Promotion
'Exalt her, and she will promote you' (Proverbs 4:8)

12. Healing and good health
'For they *are* life to those who find them, and health to all their flesh'
(Proverbs 4:22)

Epilogue: Wisdom for Life

Benjamin Franklin once said, 'The doors of wisdom are never shut.' Wisdom is always crying out to us – at the gates, at the entrance of the doors, on top of the hill, at the crossroads where the two paths meet.

Even when you find yourself walking down the wrong path, wisdom will be shouting out loudly to direct you to make the right choices. It is simply a matter of tuning your ear to hear it – and then applying it to your life.

The best way I can describe wisdom is God's Word applied. When Jesus was tempted and challenged by Satan in the wilderness for forty days and nights, He answered by applying the Word: 'It is written, "Man shall not live by bread alone, but by every word of God."' (Luke 4:4)

When you face temptations and challenges, how do you respond? The fact is that the wisdom of God provides the answers to life's impossible questions.

The Bible contains the wealth of wisdom that relates to every circumstance you may face in your life – your family, your finances, your career, your inner peace. No wonder Solomon urges us:

'Keep her [wisdom], for she *is* your life.' (Proverbs 4:13)

Wisdom is the key to the kind of life you may only dream about. I pray that you will choose wisdom, build your life upon the principles of God and see His benefits across the spectrum of your life.

May you live a great life in Him!
Brian Houston

BOOK FIVE

HOW TO LIVE IN HEALTH & WHOLENESS

Principles for health and
wholeness in body, soul and spirit

HEALTH

'For they *are* life to those who find them,
And health to all their flesh.' (Proverbs 4:22)

\HEALTH\, n. [OE. helthe]
hale, sound, whole. [See 'whole'.]
1. The state of being hale, sound, or whole,
in body, mind, or soul; especially, the
state of being free from physical disease
or pain. (Webster's Revised Unabridged
Dictionary)

How to Live in Health

'...give attention to my words... For they *are* life to those who
find them, and health to all their flesh.' (Proverbs 4:20,22)

Health is a gift from God - a great and sometimes underestimated gift
from God. Good health has been a very real friend to God's plans and
purposes for my life. Undoubtedly, this is why the Apostle John of the
New Testament, declared 'prosperity and good health' to be his greatest
wish for his good friend, Gaius.

Do you believe good health is God's will for your life? I most definitely do!
My first experience of healing was at the age of six. My mother heard strange
noises coming from my bedroom and ran in to find me unconscious and
blue. The doctor came urgently and suggested that, without improvement,
I should be transferred by ambulance to the hospital. He was so concerned
that he came twice more during the night, but my parents prayed fervently,
and trusted God. To the family doctor's amazement, the following morning
I woke up and told my father I was 'starving,' and asked for some Weet-Bix,
before running outside to play.

Time and again, over the years I have seen God's hand of healing in
people's lives. How much value do you place on your health and well-
being? There are a multitude of resources available on the subject of
health, including materials on diet, exercise, spiritual healing, medical
advice and natural alternatives. I am sure these vary in effectiveness, but I
believe the foundational keys we require to live a healthy life are contained
in one book – the Bible. God's will for you is health and He has given you
a comprehensive manual, filled with His Divine wisdom for health and
wholeness. God's promise is this:

> '...give attention to my words; incline your ear to my sayings... for
> they *are* life to those who find them, and health to all their flesh.'
> (Proverbs 4:20,22)

I would imagine that the greatest gift you could offer someone struggling
with sickness or pain is their health. My hope is that these pages will help
you discover Bible principles that will help you live the way that God
intended: in health and wholeness!

Created for Health and Wholeness

'I will praise You, for I am fearfully *and*
wonderfully made;' (Psalm 139:14)

The first chapter of the Bible declares that God made you and me in His own image. Knowing this helps us to understand why David expressed his gratitude to the Creator by saying:

'I will praise You, for I am fearfully *and* wonderfully made;
Marvelous are Your works,
And *that* my soul knows very well.' (Psalm 139:14)

I have often joked that Bobbie, my wife, is 'wonderfully' made, and me? Well, I'm 'fearfully' made! I certainly do know that God's handiwork is marvellous. He used His own image as the blueprint in creating us. Imagine that! We are made in the image of a God of three distinct yet interconnected parts – Father, Son, and Holy Spirit. Similarly, He made us in three inseparable parts – spirit, soul and body.

Each part has the potential to impact the others either positively or negatively. Medical science recognises that pain or injury in one area can significantly impact the other two areas. Research has found emotional or psychological problems can result in physical symptoms, and vice versa. In the same way, I believe what we face spiritually can also be outworked physically and emotionally. Don't underestimate the impact your health can have on the quality of your life. Remember, you are alive to serve God and poor health can stifle your capacity to do so.

The dictionary defines health in terms of wholeness in body, mind, or soul. It goes beyond the physical and this holistic approach embraces every aspect of our lives, including building healthy relationships and healthy attitudes.

Throughout the centuries, artists and sculptors have attempted to capture the wonder of the human body, and we live at a time where people aspire to physical perfection. This causes many to worship the creation rather than the Creator. In the 21st century, genetic scientists are attempting to clone what God originally designed, yet they can only fall short of the workmanship of the Master craftsman. As the psalmist writes:

'It *is* He *who* has made us, and not we ourselves;' (Psalm 100:3)

Made in His image, the human body was created to function effectively in perfect health and in a perfect environment. That was before the fall when Man became separated from God. But the work of Jesus on the Cross reversed the curse, and because of Him, we can live in health and wholeness today.

He Died So We Could Live

'He *was* wounded for our transgressions...' (Isaiah 53:5)

The life of Jesus Christ has been depicted many times in art, music and literature, but Mel Gibson's movie 'The Passion of the Christ' stands out as one of the most graphic and deeply impacting portrayals of the hours leading up to Jesus' death. The Gospel of John clearly stated the purpose:

> 'For God so loved the world that He gave His only begotten Son, that whoever believes in Him should not perish but have everlasting life.' (John 3:16)

The Crucifixion is the most significant act of love the world has ever seen, yet so many never fully grasp what Jesus did for us then. Many believers understand that He died for our sins so we could have eternal life, but the work of the Cross also purchased wholeness and healing for our physical life on earth. Centuries before Christ's death, the prophet Isaiah wrote:

> 'But He *was* wounded for our transgressions,
> *He was* bruised for our iniquities;
> The chastisement for our peace *was* upon Him,
> And by His stripes we are healed.' (Isaiah 53:5)

The Roman custom of scourging prisoners involved a whip with one or more lashes which often had pieces of wire or sharp bone attached to each strand. As each lash tore at His flesh, the stripes on the body of Jesus were for the healing of us all.

Isaiah's words are powerful: 'By His stripes, we are healed.' It doesn't refer to healing in the past (i.e. we were healed) but it is written in the present tense, declaring we are healed – physically, emotionally and spiritually! During His earthly life, Jesus encountered many who were sick and He healed them. The Bible says: 'And great multitudes followed Him, and He healed them all.' (Matthew 12:15) Yet healing was not limited to the touch of Jesus 2,000 years ago. On the Cross, Jesus paid the price for the greatest antidote to ill-health and brokenness for us today.

Life and Death

'I have come that they may have life, and that they
may have *it* more abundantly.' (John 10:10)

'Loving God, loving people, loving life' is one of the defining themes of
Hillsong Church. It expresses our personal passion to build a *healthy* church
full of *healthy* people who have a *healthy* relationship with God.

Visitors to our church often remark on the spirit of life that prevails there.
'It is so positive,' some are heard to say. This particularly stands out to those
whose perception of church is a place that is dead and lifeless. Sadly, there
are some churches that were once thriving places of worship but have
degenerated to a state of ill-health. Somewhere along the line they began
to lose the spark of life.

The analogy between the Church and a human body is scriptural, yet
the 'body of Christ' was never meant to represent a dead, lifeless corpse.
Instead, we should reflect a body that is pulsating with life, energy and
creativity – the image of the very Source of life Himself.

Jesus is synonymous with life. Everything about Him points towards
healing and wholeness but there are some who blame God for their ill-
health. I have never found scripture that says His will for us is sickness.
On the contrary, Jesus said: 'The thief does not come except to steal, and
to kill, and to destroy. I have come that they may have life, and that they
may have *it* more abundantly.' (John 10:10)

The elements of an abundant life don't include suffering or sickness. Death
and destruction is the desire of the devil. Jesus referred to him as a 'thief'
and he will always try to rob us of the life God intends for us.

During our lives, we will find ourselves facing the health hazards the
devil throws our way. These could be attacks against our physical bodies,
emotions, relationships, and even our churches.

The good news is that God has ensured that we are well equipped and positioned to win. The Bible provides us with the wisdom we need to sustain health and life across the spectrum of our lives.

Healing

'The Sun of Righteousness shall arise
With healing in His wings...' (Malachi 4:2)

\ HEAL \
v. healed, healing, heals
1. To restore to health or soundness; cure.
2. To set right; repair.
3. To restore (a person) to spiritual wholeness.
(The American Heritage Dictionary of the English Language)

What do You Believe About Healing?

'For I *am* the LORD who heals you.' (Exodus 15:26)

I have been preaching, teaching, and pastoring for many years now. During that time I have seen how a person's belief shapes their reality. God's will for us to be in health is opposed by the devil's goal to keep us contained through sickness and suffering. Unfortunately, some people accept beliefs about God and sickness that simply are not true. They end up living at the level of their belief and never know the fullness of God's blessing.

It saddens me when suffering people are told their illness is God's will because He wants to teach them a lesson, or that sickness is a result of sin in their life. If that were true, we would all be dead, because we are all sinners! I have met people who were told they weren't healed because they didn't have enough faith.' Such 'diagnoses' replace hope with hopelessness, guilt or condemnation.

The book of Job tells of his darkest days. In a time of great suffering, he was surrounded by well-intentioned friends who really were more of a hindrance than a help. One said there must be something wrong with Job or God would have healed him by now. Another told Job to accept his suffering as 'God's will.' After forty-one chapters, and with much discussion and dialogue among these so-called 'comforters', Job finally concluded:

'I know that You can do everything,
And that no purpose *of Yours* can be withheld from You.' (Job 42:2)

The outcome was that God restored Job's health and he was granted twice as much as he had before. He went on to live to a ripe old age and 'the LORD blessed the latter *days* of Job more than his beginning'. (Job 42:12)

A foundational key to good health is a revelation that God is our healer. Instead of lowering your beliefs to the level of your experience, I encourage you to rise above circumstances and stand firm on your beliefs. No matter what the outcome, believe and trust Him when He says: 'I *am* the LORD who heals you.' (Exodus 15:26)

Equipped for Health

'For the weapons of our warfare *are* not carnal
but mighty in God...' (2 Corinthians 10:4)

One certainty about life is that we will face challenges. It could be a fight for our health, a battle in our minds, or even contending for our spiritual well-being. In these times we need to have the spirit of an overcomer rather than be overwhelmed or ruled by our situation. This involves a determination to rise up and take hold of what is rightfully ours.

The Apostle Paul used the analogy of a war: 'For though we walk in the flesh, we do not war according to the flesh. For the weapons of our warfare *are* not carnal but mighty in God for pulling down strongholds,' (2 Corinthians 10:3-4)

When doing battle for our health, there are spiritual weapons readily available to us. The greatest of these is prayer. Prayer has the power to change circumstances and situations. James wrote: '...and pray for one another, that you may be healed. The effective, fervent prayer of a righteous man avails much.' (James 5:16)

Prayer changes things. A study of the life of Jesus will reveal that prayer was the source of His strength. When facing any major situation, Jesus would take time to pray. For example, in the Garden of Gethsemane before He was arrested, Jesus steeled Himself in prayer to physically endure the Cross. The Lord has provided the means for our healing in many different ways and on various levels. In my own experience, I have witnessed God's healing power numerous times through each of the following:

1. Nature
2. Medicine
3. Faith
4. Miracles

In the following pages, we will examine each of these and see how we can gain His promise of health and wholeness in our own lives.

Natural Healing

'You made all the delicate, inner parts of my body and knit
me together in my mother's womb.' (Psalm 139:13 NLT)

Like every adventurous young boy, I had my share of accidents and injuries
while growing up – broken toes, broken fingers and I even broke an ankle
whilst tobogganing on a sheet of corrugated iron! Remarkably though,
today I am still in one piece. Wounds that needed stitching (and a trip
to the casualty ward) have healed; torn muscles and broken bones have
knitted together. The Bible says, 'For You formed my inward parts;' (Psalm
139:13) 'you knit me together in my mother's womb.' (Psalm 139:13 NIV)

God created the human body with the ability to heal and repair itself.
I believe this is one of the ways God has made provision for our health
and healing. Our immune system is designed to naturally counteract the
effects of sickness or injury. You don't have to think about it – your body
naturally works towards health and healing.

The Ancient Greek physician, Hippocrates, observed this too. He said,
'Natural forces within us are the true healers of disease.' The capacity of
the human body to recover is certainly remarkable but don't leave your
physical health to chance. We live on a planet which is governed by natural
laws, such as the law of gravity. You know, what goes up, must come down.
As we get older, the impact of gravity on our ageing bodies becomes more
and more obvious.

Then there is the second law of thermodynamics, or the law of entropy,
which states that everything is proceeding toward a state of greater disorder
or decay. Left to their own devices, our physical bodies inevitably tend
towards decay. Friend, if you don't manage your health, you may end up
managing a health crisis. Unfortunately, you can only do so much about
the natural ageing process, but if you will invest into your own well-being
(spirit, soul and body), the best years of your life may well be ahead of you.

Be encouraged by the words of the Apostle Paul: 'Therefore we do not lose
heart. Even though our outward *man* is perishing, yet the inward man is
being renewed day by day.' (2 Corinthians 4:16)

God Uses People

'Those who are well have no need of a physician,
but those who are sick.' (Luke 5:31)

A doctor named Luke wrote one of the most detailed accounts of Christ's life and ministry. I find it interesting that a man whose profession involved healing, felt so compelled to research and document the life of history's greatest Healer. Luke wrote in his Gospel, 'Jesus answered and said to them, "Those who are well have no need of a physician, but those who are sick."' (Luke 5:31)

I have no problem believing that God can use medical professionals to heal us because that is what God does – He uses people. He doesn't have to, but He chooses to. He can use people to minister life and health to you in the same way that He uses people to establish His Church on the earth.

Some see modern medicine as a contradiction to their faith, but I don't believe this is so. A doctor's diagnosis or prescription has saved many a life, and let us not forget Jesus' stated purpose: He came to give us life, both now and in eternity.

Five centuries before the birth of Christ, Hippocrates radically influenced popular medical beliefs. Up until that time, the main cause of illness was considered to be demonic possession or evil spirits, but Hippocrates introduced a scientific approach. His main emphasis was to build up a patient's strength through diet and hygiene. While the Bible does cite demons as responsible for certain conditions, it is obviously not always the case. Often, a practical approach to health is what is needed.

The Hippocratic Oath still sets the ethical standards for medical practitioners today. Hippocrates wasn't a Christian but he recognised there was a spiritual side to healing. He wrote, 'Prayer indeed is good, but while calling on the gods a man should himself lend a hand.' (Hippocrates, Regimen). Thank God for dedicated people who have studied medicine and devoted their lives to alleviating or healing the pain of others. They are helping people enjoy what God intended for them – health and wholeness.

Faith for Healing
'Your faith has made you well.' (Luke 17:19)

Have you ever received a negative health report? It can certainly come as a shock, but how you respond is all important. This is where faith gets involved. You have the diagnosis but now, what are you going to believe? Despite a bad report, you can still believe that God's will for your life is health and wholeness.

Faith is so important in the pursuit of supernatural healing. Our church, Hillsong Church, is committed to praying for the sick. We believe through faith in God, people can be healed. The Bible makes this clear, 'the prayer of faith will save the sick, and the Lord will raise him up.' (James 5:15) Every week we receive praise reports and testimonies from those whose prayers have been answered. If someone isn't healed in the way we expect, I am not going stop believing God's Word, the Bible. Bringing our belief down to the level of our experience will never help. We should do exactly the opposite. Commit to lifting your experience to the level of your belief!

Some cynics would say that encouraging faith in God for healing is giving people 'false hope', but I believe some hope is better than no hope at all. Even the secular proverb professes, 'Where there is life, there is hope'! Faith connects you with God's will for your life. Jesus made the following statement on several occasions, 'Your faith has made you well.' (Matthew 9:22; Mark 10:52; Luke 17:19)

When He healed blind Bartimaeus, the woman haemmoraging blood and one of ten lepers, Jesus remarked on their faith. He also marvelled at the faith of a Roman centurion who believed his servant would be healed and spoke of 'such great faith' (Matthew 8:10).

Your faith is crucial to health and healing, but it must never become an issue of guilt or condemnation. Christians should never judge another's level of faith. To say that a lack of faith prevented someone's healing is a judgmental and ungodly attitude. Rather than judging or preaching at sick people, our love and compassion should shine through. We should 'rejoice with those who rejoice, and weep with those who weep'. (Romans 12:15)

Miracles
'...power went out from Him and healed *them* all.' (Luke 6:19)

There is something deep within humanity that is fascinated by the supernatural. The Book of Luke describes multitudes flocking to Jesus because news had spread of His miraculous works.

> 'And the whole multitude sought to touch Him, for power went out from Him and healed *them* all.' (Luke 6:19)

We live in a world that craves instant gratification. When we get sick, we want an immediate cure. Amazingly, people desire the miraculous; yet struggle to accept the God of miracles in their day-to-day lives. Some theologians and churchgoers believe miracles were performed through Jesus and the Apostles in Bible times. They may also believe in a supernatural hereafter. They just don't believe that God is still doing miracles today, and I think that is tragic!

A miracle is an event that 'appears inexplicable by the laws of nature and so is held to be supernatural in origin or an act of God' (American Heritage Dictionary). It is a force that works above the laws and limitations of nature. A miracle occurs when God speeds up the process of time or accomplishes what is naturally impossible. Without doubt, miracles reveal God's supernatural intervention and they bring glory to Him.

We may be limited by the confines of the physical, natural world but through Him, we can experience the supernatural in every aspect of our lives. The work of the Cross brings supernatural healing. Not only can we obtain physical healing from sickness and disease, but broken hearts are healed, as are broken relationships, emotions and even finances.

We serve a God of miracles, and believing in Him means we must believe it all. That is, all His promises, which are ours because of the death and resurrection of Jesus. I believe God is able to perform supernatural miracles in your life. No matter what challenges you are facing, never forget that the Bible states: 'For with God nothing will be impossible.' (Luke 1:37)

WHOLENESS

'His ruling authority will grow, and there'll
be no limits to the wholeness he brings.'
(Isaiah 9:7 The Message)

\WHOLE"NESS \, n.
The quality or state of being whole,
entire, or so sound; entireness; totality;
completeness. (Webster's Revised
Unabridged Dictionary)

Do You Want to be Made Whole?

'Wilt thou be made whole?' (John 5:6 KJV)

With wholeness comes change. A person who is physically whole can walk, run, jump or skip. To be emotionally whole means you can love, forgive, speak positively and have hope. Spiritual wholeness signifies you are changing, growing and are positioned to live life purposefully.

Some 2,000 years ago, Jesus encountered a man who had been an invalid for 38 years. He spent his days lying next to the pool of Bethesda in Jerusalem, hoping for a miracle. At certain times, it was believed an angel would stir up the water and the first person in the pool would be cured of their disease. On meeting this man, Jesus asked, 'Wilt thou be made whole?' (John 5:6 KJV)

What a strange question! This man had that condition for thirty-eight years and Jesus asked him if he wanted to be made whole! Perhaps the question was about more than physical healing. I can't help but think what Jesus was ultimately asking was this: 'Do you want to be complete? Do you really know what wholeness will mean, and the responsibility it will bring?'

Think about it. It is not easy to change after thirty-eight years in a certain condition. The fact is, if you go through life with a limp, you have a reason not to attempt a 100 metre sprint, let alone train for a marathon. The moment Jesus told the man to 'rise up and walk,' his life was about to change. There was no reason for him to return to the pool the next day. Everything would be different.

While people may think they want to be made whole, many don't want the responsibility and accountability that goes with it. Wholeness for an abused person means they are ready to forgive and move on. For a hurt person, it means they are ready to trust again.

'Do you want to be made whole?' The question is as relevant to us today as it was back at the pool of Bethesda. Are you willing to accept the changes or make the adjustments in all areas of life that wholeness may demand?

Why Wholeness is Necessary

'...He who has begun a good work in you will complete
it until the day of Jesus Christ;' (Philippians 1:6)

Imagine spending hours completing a jigsaw puzzle only to discover that there is one piece missing. What stands out – the beautiful picture or the one missing piece? Like this jigsaw puzzle, it is often one small, unresolved issue that prevents us from reaching our full potential and living life, whole.

Take the person blessed with good looks and natural talent but blighted by insecurity. They have everything they need to succeed in life, but somehow fall short of the mark. Insecurity or a low self-esteem could be the missing piece – the limitation that sabotages their personality and affects their communication, relationships, and their sense of self worth. Ultimately, this one 'missing piece' can swamp all the good qualities they are naturally blessed with.

The Apostle Paul encourages us to keep growing and expanding: '...being confident of this very thing, that He who has begun a good work in you will complete *it*...' (Philippians 1:6)

The desire to be whole and complete in body, soul and spirit should be within each of us. The Bible describes believers as 'living epistles' – people watch us because we reflect the image of the Creator. If you bought a car and it didn't function properly, it wouldn't reflect well on the manufacturer. When our lives are moving toward wholeness, it reflects well on our Maker.

Being whole means we can enjoy the abundant life Jesus spoke about. To know the fullness of life He promised, we should be willing to be accountable and take responsibility. Being whole is not just about us and our needs. When we are whole, we have the capacity to help or lift up others, and they can depend on us. So, do you want to be made whole?

Christ wants to deal with the real issues in your life so you can move forward. Instead of a band-aid mentality to Christianity, we need to allow the Holy Spirit to reveal those areas that limit us, and begin a work that will enable us to become all that God has called us to be.

A Healthy Soul

'I pray that you may prosper in all things and be
in health, just as your soul prospers.' (3 John 2)

One of my greatest priorities as a pastor is the on-going health of our church. You see, I have learned over the years that attacks from the outside don't hurt us and ultimately don't determine the well-being of the church. If the soul of our church is healthy, weapons may be formed against us but they will not prevail. The reality is that a healthy body is impacted by a healthy soul. The Apostle John wrote: 'Beloved, I pray that you may prosper in all things and be in health, just as your soul prospers.' (3 John 2)

I believe there is a direct correlation between the condition of our soul and our overall health. What is happening on the inside affects what is on the outside. The soul is like the engine room of our lives. It is the seat of our thinking, emotions and will. When the core of our being is unhealthy, it has a significant effect on everything else.

In many of the Psalms, it is evident that the writer recognised the importance of the condition of his soul. When he felt distressed on the inside, he would speak to his inner man.'Why are you cast down, O my soul? And why are you disquieted within me? Hope in God; for I shall yet praise Him, the help of my countenance and my God.' (Psalm 42:11)

These words paint a picture of someone who refuses to be dictated to by unproductive feelings, negative thoughts or poor internal choices. He took command over his own soul and pointed his own inner world toward hope.

Do you want to be made whole? Take a look at the words of John: 'Dear friend, and I pray that all goes well for you. I hope that you are as strong in body, as I know you are in spirit.' (3 John 2 CEV)

Don't neglect the health of your soul because it is a foundational key for a healthy life.

The Power of the Inner Man

'My heart also instructs me in the night seasons.' (Psalm 16:7)

If it is the content of our hearts that determines the condition of our lives, surely we must dig beneath the veneer and ask ourselves the tough questions. What is really happening within me? And, what am I prepared to do about it? Here is a Proverb with some clear advice: 'For as he thinks in his heart, so *is* he.' (Proverbs 23:7)

Human nature tends to react to external things, rather than dealing with the inner issues. The devil is crafty and attempts to defeat us on the inside. He wants to attack our source of strength. The Bible says, 'The spirit of a man will sustain him in sickness, but who can bear a broken spirit?' (Proverbs 18:14) When something is broken, it doesn't function properly. If you are broken on the inside, you won't be in a strong position to withstand attacks. If you are serious about living a life of wholeness, you will give attention to the real issues of your heart.

Life will throw some night seasons our way and during these times we will be directed by our hearts. David wrote, 'My heart also instructs me in the night seasons.' (Psalm 16:7)

Many things breed in the dark, including confusion or disorientation. You can lose your way in the darkness of night and have no clue which way to turn. I have seen people completely lose their way during dark or difficult times, and others who have emerged victoriously. Why do some make it through?

When you don't know which way to turn, your heart is going to guide you; it can only instruct according to what it knows. If your heart is geared toward panic, it will guide you accordingly, whereas, with the right thinking and attitudes, your heart can keep you on course. Just as a plane flies according to the way its computer is set, our lives will fly according to the way our hearts are set. Sadly, some people lose their way in a night season and never find their way back. Do you want to be made whole? Perhaps the key lies in the content of your own heart.

Changing the Condition of Your Soul

'Marvellous are Your works, and *that* my
soul knows very well.' (Psalm 139:14)

Personal trainers can help you change the condition of your physical body but how can you change the condition of your soul? It will take some commitment and discipline, but here are five ways you can begin to build health on the inside.

1. Teach your soul when to be quiet
'My soul, wait silently for God alone,' (Psalm 62:5) Many conflicting voices can dictate what happens on the inside. King David was always quick to silence other voices by instructing his soul to focus on the Lord. He commanded everything within him to bless the Lord. He was telling every conflicting emotion to be quiet!

2. Educate your soul
'...it is not good *for* a soul *to be* without knowledge,' (Proverbs 19:2)Some pursue intellectual knowledge in order to build their lives, but fail to see the value of educating their soul. You can have degrees or doctorates but ultimately, it is what your soul knows that will direct the course of your life – positively or negatively!

3. Fill your soul with hope
'This *hope* we have as an anchor of the soul, both sure and steadfast...' (Hebrews 6:19) Without hope, we have nothing to anchor or secure ourselves to when we are tossed by the storms of life. Those consumed by despair and hopelessness find themselves unhinged and then quickly drift off course. You can keep hope alive and strong by daily meditating on God's Word.

4. Teach your soul to boast
'My soul shall make its boast in the LORD;' (Psalm 34:2) Those who need to boast about themselves display all the evidence of insecurity. You can develop a different type of boast though, by boasting in the Lord: 'How good is God?' or 'My hope is in the name of the Lord!'

5. Teach your soul to be accountable

Blaming others or our circumstances is typical of human nature. Excuses only give us reason to stay the way we are. Building a healthy soul starts with accepting responsibility and accountability for our own lives.

WELL-BEING

'And the LORD our God commanded us to
obey all these laws and to fear Him for our
own prosperity and well-being...'
(Deuteronomy 6:24 NLT)

\WELL-BEING \, n.
The state of being happy and healthy and
prosperous. (Wordnet)

Making Health Your Priority
'Like fish taken in a cruel net, like birds
caught in a snare...' (Ecclesiastes 9:12)

God has blessed me with good health! Without it, I doubt I could have done all I have been able to do during my many years of ministry and continuous travel. I receive many invitations from churches and conferences all over the world. With the rigours of constant international travel, the challenge of leading a large staff, church, college and movement, you can imagine that my health has been essential.

Health should be our priority when we are well, not only when we are sick. Prevention is better than cure. It makes sense to look after ourselves rather than sap our strength struggling with ongoing health issues. The Bible says:

> 'Like fish taken in a cruel net,
> Like birds caught in a snare,
> So the sons of men *are* snared in an evil time,
> When it falls suddenly upon them.' (Ecclesiastes 9:12)

Instead of swimming with ease the way God intended, a fish caught in a net will use all its energy and resources to attempt to break free. It is the same for a bird caught in a snare. It flaps itself to exhaustion with the hope of flying again. Sadly, we can spend a lot of energy and resource trying to regain our health. Human nature means we are inclined to take good health for granted until we lose it.

Making good health a priority is not vanity. In the context of living with God-given purpose, health is a commitment to longevity and effectiveness. This is why we need to keep in good shape. If the devil can inhibit us physically, or lead us into a depressed emotional state, he will. Avoiding his snares puts us in a much stronger position to help others.

Those who get emotionally entangled in various situations can end up needing help themselves. Determine to break free of the nets and snares that could potentially ensnare you, in order to live life fully and effectively. In the words of Jesus: 'If the Son makes you free, you shall be free indeed.' (John 8:36)

Roots of Bitterness

'...if the Son makes you free, you shall be free indeed.' (John 8:36)

Sickness seems to strike randomly and it is certainly not based on what we deserve. There are various reasons why we fall ill. Statistics suggest that thirty-eight per cent of all cancers are related to diet and lifestyle. Some would believe it is more.

Undoubtedly, poor attitudes and negative emotions are key contributors to ill-health. Deep-seated anxiety, grief or resentment often results in severe physical consequences. There is evidence that some ailments have direct links to unforgiveness or bitterness, while stress can also have severe repercussions. The Bible warns, 'looking carefully... lest any root of bitterness springing up cause trouble, and by this many become defiled'. (Hebrews 12:15)

Unresolved negative emotions will have an adverse affect on your general well-being. Trouble is the result of unforgiveness. It will punish you, not the perpetrator or the cause of your pain. The writer to the Hebrews was well aware of the destruction that a hardened heart can bring. He wrote, 'Do not harden your hearts as in the rebellion, in the day of trial in the wilderness'. (Hebrews 3:8)

A hard heart locks out God, locks out others, refuses to trust, and cannot be penetrated. It is no longer theory that our emotions can affect our health. It is a medical fact. It is crucial that you deal with bitterness at its roots and maintain a free, or unblocked, spirit. The Apostle Paul said, '"Be angry, and do not sin": do not let the sun go down on your wrath'. (Ephesians 4:26)

The key is to deal immediately with the issues that confront you. Every time the sun goes down in the evening, it will rise again in the morning. If it sets on unresolved issues, it will carry them into a new day. For some people, the sun is completely shaded by yesterday's issues. They are living with the physical, emotional or spiritual fallout of years of unchecked emotions. I have chosen not to allow unproductive emotions to fester or put their roots down in my spirit. I encourage you to do the same. Choose to forgive in order to live free from bondage, brokenness and ill-health.

What a Worry
'Be anxious for nothing...' (Philippians 4:6)

Have you ever heard anyone claim they were sick with worry? Perhaps this is closer to the truth than many people realise. I once taught a series of messages called, 'What a worry, worry is!' – and it is! Anxiety is a genuine health hazard. It dulls the senses, destroys objectivity and can affect you physically, emotionally and spiritually. The Bible warns us of the consequences of worry in the inner man: 'Anxiety in the heart of man causes depression...' (Proverbs 12:25)

We can allow our minds to take us down a path of negative possibilities. Everything becomes magnified, perspective is lost and we start focusing on worst case scenarios. There is nothing to be gained by this. When depression pervades the heart, it affects your whole outlook on life. Another proverb says: 'Hope deferred makes the heart sick...' (Proverbs 13:12)

We know that the issues of life spring from the heart, and that a sick heart will have ramifications on our general well-being. To tackle this, we need to take on God's thinking. He says: 'For I know the thoughts I think toward you, says the LORD, thoughts of peace and not of evil, to give you a future and a hope.' (Jeremiah 29:11)

It is in the midst of a challenge that you find out whether you really trust Him with your future. There have been occasions when I have found myself worrying more than could be deemed healthy. I felt the effects in my neck and back, and have even lost my voice because of it.

Worrying is about trusting in your own ability. The Apostle Paul tells us how to respond to anxiety:

> 'Be anxious for nothing, but in everything by prayer and supplication, with thanksgiving, let your requests be made known to God; and the peace of God, which surpasses all understanding, will guard your hearts and minds through Christ Jesus.' (Philippians 4:6-7)

The key is to turn worry into thanksgiving. The Bible doesn't tell us to thank Him for everything but to give thanks in everything. In the midst of a worrying situation, find something to thank Him for. Replace anxiety with that internal peace that surpasses all understanding. God's peace is like a mental guard or protective shield for your heart.

A Merry Heart

'A merry heart does good, *like* medicine...' (Proverbs 17:22)

How many senses do you have? Five? Let a hearty sense of humour become the sixth! We can take life far too seriously, but there is nothing like a belly laugh to lift the spirits and give a healthy perspective on life.

The Bible speaks of humour as one of life's greatest medications:

'A merry heart does good, *like* medicine,
But a broken spirit dries the bones.' (Proverbs 17:22)

Another translation says:

'A cheerful disposition is good for your health;
gloom and doom leave you bone-tired.'
(Proverbs 17:22 The Message)

Research has proven this to be true. Not only is a cheerful spirit good for your health, but it also impacts your surroundings. A house filled with laughter will be a healthy home; a great sense of humour in a relationship will aid a healthy marriage and a congregation with a merry heart is a sign of a healthy church.

I have often said that church should be enjoyed, not endured. Sadly, some churches take themselves far too seriously. I believe that Christians should be the happiest of all people – and maybe the funniest! The life and soul of the party.

Psalm 100:2 has been a key verse in the culture of our church. It says: 'Serve the LORD with gladness;'

This refers to our spirit and attitude, and for good reason – a merry heart enables us to serve Him with greater energy and health. American author Mark Twain recognised the power of laughter when he said: 'The human race has one really effective weapon, and that is laughter.'

A free and happy spirit will impact the quality of your life and help you ride through the tough times. Weapons may be formed against our health and well-being, but we can fight back with a merry heart. My motto is 'love God, love people, and love life.'

'Happy *are* the people whose God *is* the LORD!' (Psalm 144:15)

Dealing with Dependencies

'In the world you will have tribulation; but be of good
cheer, I have overcome the world.' (John 16:33)

An unexpected blessing that has come from pastoring Hillsong Church, is the opportunity to be an unofficial 'chaplain' and friend to some key people in sport, entertainment and other high-profile roles. It has given me insight into the pressures, temptations and demands that come with a public profile. Unfortunately, history tells of many in similar positions who shattered incredible opportunities through excess or unhealthy dependencies because they didn't have the right foundation.

We all face challenges in life, and we too can become trapped in a cycle of excess or dependency in an attempt to cope. The public fallout may be greater for people of profile but the toll on our well-being is the same, regardless of who we are.

When the going gets tough, where do you turn? We were created to be dependent beings – dependent on a loving God as our source of strength, rather than in bondage to addictions. The Bible says:

'Trust in the LORD with all your heart,
And lean not on your own understanding;' (Proverbs 3:5)

Human nature is more inclined towards being 'in-dependent' or relying on our own strength instead of leaning on Him. Sadly, it is pursuits outside God's parameters that can develop into destructive dependencies. The result is addictions or obsessive behaviour that can overshadow every sphere of life.

The Bible describes the body as a 'temple of the Holy Spirit'. You cannot abuse your physical body and expect to function effectively through the journey of life. In a way, we are all like elite athletes running a race. The Apostle Paul used this analogy:

'Do you not know that those who run in a race all run, but one receives the prize? Run in such a way that you may obtain *it*. And everyone who competes *for the prize* is temperate in all things ...' (1 Corinthians 9:24-25)

Do you have temptations or weaknesses with the potential to rob you of your prize? If the prize is measured in health, happiness, family, friends, and successfully fulfilling God's will for your life, you need to challenge, starve or cut off any excess or dependency that threatens them. Do whatever it takes! The only dependency that will ultimately breathe life into your health and well-being is dependency on the Lord Jesus Christ.

BALANCE

'Do you know how the clouds are balanced
[and poised in the heavens], the wonderful
works of Him Who is perfect in knowledge?'
(Job 37:16 AMP)

\ BALANCE \, n.
4. The state of being in equipoise;
equilibrium; even adjustment; steadiness.
(Webster's Revised Unabridged Dictionary)

Source of Health and Harm

'...eat honey because *it is* good, and the honeycomb
which is sweet to your taste;' (Proverbs 24:13)

I don't believe the Bible is the strict book of rules and regulations that many believe it to be. With a New Testament perspective, we view the Scriptures according to all that Christ has accomplished. And He has set us up to win!

Life is best when you make wise and positive choices. These are choices which are based on the teachings of Jesus. I don't think my role as a pastor is to tell people what to do and what not to do. I want to equip them to make their own positive decisions – and the best decisions are geared toward producing positive outcomes in every area of life.

We need to be mindful that both health and harm can come from the same source. Look at this analogy of honey from the book of Proverbs: 'My son, eat honey because *it is* good, and the honeycomb *which is* sweet to your taste;' (Proverbs 24:13)

We know that honey is good and it tastes good. But one chapter later there is a caution, 'Have you found honey? Eat only as much as you need, lest you be filled with it and vomit.' (Proverbs 25:16)

Now I'm not aware that honey appears on any list of banned substances, but Solomon is clearly encouraging restraint. He is teaching that too much of a good thing can harm us. Health and moderation are partners.

Understanding that health and harm come from the same honey-jar should alert us to the need for discipline and balance. A healthy, Christ-like lifestyle is not so much abstinence-based as it is wisdom-based. The Apostle Paul understood the need for balance:

> 'Everything is permissible (allowable and lawful) for me; but not all things are helpful (good for me to do, expedient and profitable when considered with other things). Everything is lawful for me, but I will not become the slave of anything *or* be brought under its power.' (1 Corinthians 6:12 AMP)

We all have strengths and weaknesses, and it is up to us to take responsibility for our own well-being. Don't allow someone else's conviction (or lack of it) to become your downfall; and don't make lifestyle choices without regard for their impact on others.

Balance and Boundaries

'The spirit indeed *is* willing, but the flesh *is* weak.' (Matthew 26:41)

To live your life saying 'yes' to God and 'no' to sin is a recipe for good health!

'Fear the LORD and depart from evil. It will be health to your flesh,
And strength to your bones.' (Proverbs 3:7-8)

What we sow determines what we reap. I have already stated that the responsibility rests with us to make good choices. Solomon's proverb on honey encourages us to set positive boundaries for our lives. What does Solomon's 'honey' represent in your life? Excessiveness has been the ruin of many. Often, a bit of self-discipline and common sense would have prevented things from spinning out of control.

If you know you have a weakness for something, don't put yourself in an environment where such things are in abundance. This is why the company we keep is important. The Bible says: 'Bad company corrupts good character.' (1 Corinthians 15:33 NIV)

Jesus told His disciples: 'Watch and pray, lest you enter into temptation. The spirit indeed *is* willing, but the flesh *is* weak.' (Matthew 26:41)

There is a constant battle between the flesh and the spirit, and our everyday choices are contributing to one or the other. Decide you are not going to feed your weaknesses. Draw some responsible boundary lines in your relationships and across your life. Such parameters are releasing, rather than restricting, as they will promote good health.

We all face different challenges and some things are a matter of personal taste and choice. What is tempting to you may not be tempting to me. The Scriptures are filled with principles that will help you build a healthy life. The key is to be true to yourself. Live life with conviction and avoid falling into the traps of excess and obsession. As the proverb states:

'Have you found honey?

Eat only as much as you need...' (Proverbs 25:16)

Don't judge others. Remember, the Bible has as much to say about gluttony as it does about drunkenness. Moderation does not only apply to one area but should be applied across the spectrum of our lives. Don't over-indulge.

A Healthy Attitude to Food and Drink

'...for the kingdom of God is not eating and drinking, but
righteousness and peace and joy in the Holy Spirit.' (Romans 14:17)

In recent times, a lawsuit was brought against a large fast food chain in America. The complainant wanted financial compensation for years of eating their 'junk' food that he claimed resulted in obesity and subsequent health problems. The case was ultimately dismissed by the judge, who declared it was not the place of the law to protect people from their own excesses.

Taking responsibility for our choices includes what we eat and drink. We all need to fuel our bodies to function properly, but an unhealthy attitude to food or drink can be destructive. Some people turn to food to give them a pick-up when they are depressed, and others rely on alcohol to boost their poor self-image or low self-esteem. The Bible warns us about the consequences of these type of excesses:

'For the drunkard and the glutton will come to poverty...'
(Proverbs 23:21)

It is interesting that on many occasions the Scriptures speak of wine-bibbing and gluttony in the same sentence. Excessiveness in any form causes harm. At Hillsong Church, we don't impose rules about what people eat or what they drink; but we do teach the importance of moderation and wisdom.

The Bible has plenty to say about the things we consume, and the Old Testament contained numerous dietary laws. Jesus gives us a New Covenant which liberates us from regulations but, of course, that doesn't mean we should abandon wisdom. The Apostle Paul brought proper perspective:

'...for the kingdom of God is not eating and drinking, but
righteousness and peace and joy in the Holy Spirit.'
(Romans 14:17)

In the early Church, some of the Jewish believers held their dietary traditions in higher regard than accepting Gentiles into the Church. Their focus was more on regulations than on God's Kingdom. Jesus said:

> '...do not worry about your life, what you will eat or what you will drink; nor about your body, what you will put on. Is not life more than food and the body more than clothing?' (Matthew 6:25)

He went on to instruct us to seek first the Kingdom and His righteousness. To live a healthy life, we need to exercise caution and focus on the things that matter.

A Healthy Attitude to Exercise

'...do you not know that your body is the temple of the
Holy Spirit *who* is in you...?' (1 Corinthians 6:19)

It's never easy to get out of bed in the middle of winter, pull on those trackpants and jog a few kilometres in the cold morning air. But it always feels good to have done it! We live in a society that is extremely image conscious. We need to look after ourselves – body, soul and spirit – and a healthy attitude to exercise is both valuable and necessary. But of course, obsession is never healthy and balance is essential. The Bible says: 'Or do you not know that your body is the temple of the Holy Spirit *who is* in you...?' (1 Corinthians 6:19)

Our bodies need to be kept in good shape to function well. How can we fulfill the purposes of God in our lives if we neglect our bodies? There is a Spanish proverb that says, 'A man too busy to take care of his health is like a mechanic too busy to take care of his tools.'

Your body is the vehicle God has given you to carry out His purposes. He has a great plan for your life and you need to be in good health to fulfill it. You don't need your body to break down halfway into your journey. The Apostle Paul recognised this: 'But I discipline my body and bring *it* into subjection...' (1 Corinthians 9:27).

Looking after your body will add to your health and well-being. I know that I do everything better when I exercise and endeavour to be physically fit. But the honey-jar principle applies here too. Don't allow exercise and image to become an obsession that unbalances or rules your life. Paul wrote:

'For bodily exercise profits a little, but godliness is profitable for all things, having promise of the life that now is and of that which is to come.' (1 Timothy 4:8)

Paul wasn't dismissing exercise. He acknowledged its benefits but he put into perspective the area most people tend to neglect – the spiritual side of their lives. Remember to exercise those spiritual muscles as well.

A Healthy Attitude to Sex
'Flee sexual immorality.' (1 Corinthians 6:18)

The Bible presents a different moral code to the worldly lifestyle. Some may mock these principles and call them old-fashioned, but they simply give us healthy parameters in order to live life well. These parameters are not there to limit or suppress our lives but rather to bring blessing.

Sexual intimacy is a wonderful God-given gift, and it has the potential to enhance a loving relationship. Yet outside Godly principles, it can bring heartache, devastation, mistrust and brokenness.

Abuse is described as wrong or improper use; misuse: the abuse of privileges. There are many who have been devastated by the abuse of uncontrolled sexuality. What God intended to be healthy and beautiful is perverted. Trust can be broken, emotions scarred, relationships devastated, and futures affected – all because of immorality.

The Bible clearly indicates the perils of sexual immorality, using the analogy of a woman who is inviting and alluring: 'For the lips of an immoral woman drip honey' (Proverbs 5:3). This chapter of Proverbs continues to illustrate the destruction of promiscuity. Many are quickly captivated and seduced by the sweetness of the moment, without contemplating the disastrous results at the end of the road. They end up paying a massive personal cost. The Apostle Paul said, 'Flee sexual immorality.' (1 Corinthians 6:18)

His strong counsel is to run from sexual temptation. We are not taught to resist temptation – we are taught to flee from it. Don't even put yourself in a compromising position, physically or emotionally. This includes guarding your mind from the sexual images that are subtly promoted in the media. You need to know when to switch off... without delay!

Sex is good, but not when we ignore God's counsel. Marriage was His idea and is the perfect fit for a healthy sex life.

Knowing When to Rest

'I lay down and slept; I awoke, for the
LORD sustained me.' (Psalm 3:5)

The Carpenters sang, 'Rainy days and Mondays always get me down' but that's not true for me! I love Mondays. It's my day off. After multiple weekend services, expending much physical, emotional and spiritual energy, I am ready for a quiet Monday.

In the first chapter of Genesis, we are told that God Himself rested on the seventh day. To live a healthy, balanced life we need to know the value of rest. A good night's sleep equips us to serve the Lord effectively. It's His way of renewing, restoring and replenishing us. We can only keep going a certain amount of time before we lose our concentration and edge. That is, of course, unless we rest! The promise of God is this:

'When you lie down, you will not be afraid.
Yes, you will lie down and your sleep will be sweet.' (Proverbs 3:24)

Like rest and relaxation, our sleep should be a sweet reward, not ridden with fear and anxiety. I love the way in the midst of increased opposition, David was able to say:

'I lay down and slept;
I awoke, for the LORD sustained me.' (Psalm 3:5)

I lay down! I slept! I awoke! This sounds better than tossing and turning all night, then waking up ragged and exhausted. I believe for this blessing in my life. It was a good night's sleep that renewed David's strength for the challenges of a new day, but his son, Solomon, warns us against becoming sluggish. Sleep is a reward for a hard days work, yet, for some, work is an unwelcome interruption to their sleep.

'Do not love sleep, lest you come to poverty;' (Proverbs 20:13)

Some people are asleep to their potential and they miss opportunities to serve God. Life is for living, not sleeping. I love my Mondays, but their value is achieved by approaching the rest of the week with a zest for work and accomplishment. The purpose of sleep and relaxation is to re-charge us so we can live effective, purpose-filled lives. It is important to find the balance. Jesus said: 'Come to Me, all *you* who labor and are heavy laden, and I will give you rest.' (Matthew 11:28)

He spoke of work and rest in the same sentence, and ultimately the two should complement one another. Don't be striving so hard that you forget to enjoy life. In the midst of the busyness of life, we need to know when to stop and rest.

Epilogue: Leading a Healthy Example

'With long life I will satisfy him, and show
him My salvation.' (Psalm 91:16)

Undoubtedly, leadership is example. It is all about giving people something to follow. As a Church leader, I want my leadership to be seen in my marriage, my family, my finances, and across all other areas of my life.

A leader's attitude is critical in sickness and in health. My wife Bobbie and I have recently watched on as several of our close friends have confronted life threatening illnesses. Their faith and their courage have been awe-inspiring. Sometimes, it is in these very real challenges that true leadership is proven. I am committed to last the distance and to fulfil everything that God has called me to do. We all need to make our health a priority. The promise of God is this: 'With long life I will satisfy him, and show him My salvation.' (Psalm 91:16)

The devil will attempt to attack your physical, mental and spiritual well-being because he wants to render you ineffective. The truth is that if you don't manage your health, you may find yourself trying to manage a health crisis, and you don't want that!

God has given us everything needed to live life well. Through the Bible, we are given the wisdom and instruction by which we can develop a positive and productive attitude to health and wholeness. A genuinely biblical approach to health is not legalistic. With Godly wisdom, and with good parameters in place, you can enhance your well-being. I believe in divine health – Bible principles produce Bible results!

My closing prayer for you echoes the words of the Apostle John:

'I pray for good fortune in everything you do, and for your good health–that your everyday affairs prosper, as well as your soul!' (3 John 2 The Message)

Life is for living, so live it well.
The best is yet to come!
Brian Houston

ABOUT THE AUTHOR

Many pastors and ministry leaders around the world regard Pastor Brian Houston as a well-loved and influential church statesman.

Along with his wife, Bobbie, they are the Senior Pastors of Hillsong Church; a local church with several global campuses, known for it's healthy approach to Church life, Mission, Innovation, Conferences, College and Praise and Worship. The world renowned Hillsong Conference and Colour Women's Conferences are attended by tens of thousands of pastors and leaders from around the globe every year, and held in some of Sydney and London's largest arenas and stadiums.

His teaching resources and podcasts are in high demand - connecting people to biblical truths, with a unique ability to apply them to everyday issues of life. Pastor Brian's warm and yet confronting style has gained a worldwide audience through Hillsong Television, one of Hillsong Church's primary mission endeavours. Hillsong Television can be watched from nearly every nation, through traditional TV platforms and digital Internet technology.

Today, Hillsong Church is described as "One House, with many rooms." With flagship campuses in Australia, Hillsong's global congregations continue to add life and depth to this local church, with campuses in influential cities such as London, Cape Town, Kiev, Moscow, Paris, Stockholm, Germany, Amsterdam and New York City. Each Hillsong Church plant is passionate about the local communities in which they operate and place a strong emphasis on social justice and helping people both within their own city and abroad.

Today, after over 35 years of marriage, Brian and Bobbie have three adult children, a growing brood of grandchildren and MANY spiritual sons and daughters who often affectionately call him 'The Big Eagle.' (Who knows why!?) Pastor Brian lives by a conviction that 'THE BEST IS YET TO COME' and when you are around him, it's hard not to believe that that is the truth...

ABOUT THIS SERIES

HOW TO LIVE A BLESSED LIFE
Principles From The Life Of The Righteous Man In Psalm 112
Every human being should desire to live a blessed life - all we need to know is how. The unnamed man described in Psalm 112 is one who reflects the blessing of God across the spectrum of his life. In this book, Brian Houston shows how we can be blessed in every area of our lives by applying the same principles.

HOW TO BUILD GREAT RELATIONSHIPS
Principles For Friendship And Partnership, Marriage And Parenting
One of the greatest gifts God has given us is people - who add and contribute towards blessing our lives. Sadly, many never seem to succeed in building the kind of intimate relationships they long for. The second book in the Maximised Life Series, this book by Brian Houston shares the principles that can enhance some our most important relationships.

HOW TO FLOURISH IN LIFE
Principles For Building A Thriving, Productive Life
God's will is that you flourish and thrive in every area of your life. Sadly, many never realise the great potential within them. Brian Houston has committed his life to building the kind of church where people can flourish and grow as God intended. In this book, he shares the powerful principles that build thriving churches and productive lives.

HOW TO MAKE WISE CHOICES
Principles For Building A Life Of Wisdom
The fourth book in The Maximised Life Series: There are some who think the Bible is full of rules and regulations, but it is a book of wisdom that embraces the entire spectrum of life. In essence, it teaches us how to live life well. In this book, Brian Houston examines the wisdom of Solomon and how we can make choices that will build the kind of life God intends for us.

HOW TO LIVE IN HEALTH & WHOLENESS
Principles For Health & Wholeness In Body, Soul And Spirit
The fifth book in the Maximised Life Series: For some, the quest for physical perfection is an obsession. For many, health is something they take for granted until they lose it. For those struggling with sickness and disease, health is the greatest gift of all. In this book, Brian Houston examines the biblical principles relating to building a life of health and wholeness.